Will the Real Me Please Stand Up?

Discovering & Enjoying Your True Identity

Dr. Sandy Madden

Will The Real Me Please Stand Up?

Tellwell Talent
www.tellwell.ca

ISBN
978-1-77302-099-0 (Paperback)

To my husband George. I wouldn't be who I am without you.
Thank you for continually bringing the best "me" out of me.

Table of Contents

Introduction

Will the Real (person) Please Stand Up? is the catch phrase from an American television game show called *To Tell the Truth.* This program has aired in various forms since 1956 both on networks and in syndication - along with *The Price Is Right, Let's Make a Deal, The Newlywed Game,* and *Jeopardy.*

The show features a panel of four celebrities whose objective is the correct identification of a described contestant who has an unusual occupation or experience. This central character is accompanied by two impostors who pretend to be the central character. Together, the three persons are said to belong to a "team of challengers".

The celebrity panelists question the three contestants. The impostors are allowed to lie, but the central character swears "to tell the truth". Following the questioning period, the panel votes to identify who of the three challengers is telling the truth and is thus the central character. Once the votes are in, the host asks, *"Will the real [person's name] please stand up?"* The central character then stands and the imposters are left seated.*1*

In addition to being both humorous and entertaining, the program illustrates the fact that the true identity of an individual can be obscured by deception and manipulation. This book is designed to help you sift through all the lies you have believed about yourself, to break free from any manipulation you have been trapped in, and to open your eyes to who you really are - an amazing, powerful, and uniquely gifted individual. However, unlike the TV program where other people work to uncover an identity, we will be working personally to uncover our own true selves.

This book is not another self-help, five steps to success manual. Though there is a place for these types of behavioural modification guides, this book goes beyond external behaviour to the internal motivation behind the behaviour. If we never solidify the foundation of our self-worth, everything external that we build upon this weak foundation will be flawed.

Ultimately, we are who we believe ourselves to be. Our behaviour is shaped by our self-assumptions. This book is meant to challenge your beliefs, expose the lies that have limited you, and help you discover the extraordinary person you really are.

Ultimately, we are who we believe ourselves to be.

Ironically, though this is not a "success" book, discovering your true identity will unlock the passion, creativity, and personal growth that create success. Success is the fruit - our self-worth or identity is the tree that produces the fruit. When we take care of the tree, the fruit comes naturally.

We all have implanted within us a seed of identity. This seed, like every other, contains the necessary DNA to flourish. However, the seed must be in the right conditions for this to happen or it will remain dormant.

And unfortunately, in this world of brokenness, many of us have less than ideal conditions for our seeds to flourish. That is why I'm so passionate about this subject - I want to help people to cultivate those precious seeds within them and hopefully bypass some of the pain I've gone through in this area.

I've spent most of my life trying to figure out who I am. I've struggled to feel good about myself and wore myself out trying to gain acceptance. One of my earliest and most painful memories of a personal identity crisis was as a young girl exploring the attic of my house. I was in a fanciful reverie as I discovered a box that contained my baby-book complete with a soft, fine lock of my hair from my first haircut. I smiled in wonder as I held up the tiny sleeper that I had worn on the day I came home from the hospital.

But the joy and wonder ended abruptly when my eyes fell upon a piece of scrap paper folded at the bottom of the box. When I unfolded it I saw a list of boys' names written gracefully, with my name scratched at the bottom. For a moment I contemplated what those boys' names would be doing in my baby book? Then all at once it hit me like a steel-toed kick in the gut... my parents had wanted a boy but instead they got me - another girl.

I never had the courage to confront my parents or even speak about my "discovery". It was a wound I carried silently within me that spawned all manner of self-hatred and negative behaviour which I will talk about in more detail throughout the book.

Right now, your life may seem barren and nothing is growing. The good news is that if you're alive, there's hope! You're not dead - you're only dormant. Many species of plants have seeds that delay germination for many months or even years. Some seeds can remain in the soil for more than fifty years before germination. 2

Be encouraged! All the potential for you to flourish is still in you. All you need to do is provide the right conditions and the real you, like that seed, will spring to life.

The old saying, *"You can count the seeds in an apple but you can't count the apples in a seed"* holds a great truth. Nobody can measure the potential of a seed. Likewise, nobody can measure the potential of the person that lies within you.

As you read this book, I believe that the sleeping seed of identity and self-discovery within you will be awakened and will open a whole new world of possibilities for you. In addition, you will be given the practical tools you need to reach your maximum potential.

Welcome to the first step in the most rewarding journey of your life - discovering and enjoying your true identity.

1. CHAPTER ONE

WHO AM I ANYWAY?

"Who we are is where happiness lies, but this is so often blocked by who we have become." 1

Dr. Caroline Leaf

You may be familiar with a popular TV show called *Whose Line is it Anyway?* This is a satire where actors are required to improvise random and often ludicrous stunts and dialogue in hopes of winning the bogus "prize" at the end of the show. Their role as performers is that they model any number of assigned identities for the entertainment of the audience.

The old Shakespearian saying, *"All the world's a stage"* is tragically accurate. As if we are playing an assigned role on *Whose Line is it Anyway,* we often feel compelled to act out of our true character and even perform ludicrous stunts in hopes of gaining the approval of our "audience".

Have you ever found yourself in a place where you don't really feel you can be yourself? You know what I mean: those awkward social gatherings where all the successful people come together to discuss their latest and greatest achievements - those places where you feel insignificant and your insecurities flare.

Because it's a formal event, you dig out that outfit at the back of your closest reserved for such occasions. As you struggle to do up the straining zipper, you are convinced the outfit must have shrunk since the last time you wore it. Suffocating from the strangling waistline and the anticipation of the stuffed-shirt event, you head out the door. When you arrive, you desperately scan the room looking for a friendly face, only to find you are assigned a seat across from an intimidating, beautiful, and immaculately dressed woman whose eyes seem to look right through you when she asks, "So what do you do?"

If you're like me, you feel the hot rush of blood pumping to your already frazzled brain as you stammer something intelligent like, "Uhhh, I'm a psychopath, I mean a psychotherapist." Then you begin the frantic process of trying to legitimize yourself in the face of this obviously "superior" individual who seems to be measuring your every word and finding you falling seriously short of the elusive "mark".

Compare this abysmal feeling to the comforting feeling you have when you're with your closest friend. This is the place where you can truly be "yourself". You can wear your baggy sweats and your comfy old slippers while you veg on the couch with a bowl of popcorn, watching your favourite movie. Conversation is easy and relaxed. You are free to express your fears, your dreams, your anger, and your love without fear of rejection or judgment.

Unfortunately we can't live our entire lives only interacting with the people that we feel comfortable being ourselves with. We must deal with all kinds of less than sympathetic people - everyone from the border patrol officer to our overbearing mother-in-law; from our ex-spouse to our micro-managing boss.

In a conflicting world, how can we do like Shakespeare so wisely advises in his play *Hamlet*?

"This above all: To thine own self be true."

In order to be true to ourselves, we need to know who we are. Our identity is not something we decide in a moment; rather, it is something we discover over time. This book is written to help you discover the real you that is often buried deep inside. Like a long-forgotten treasure hidden in a deep dark cave, you can use the principles in this book like a treasure map to unearth and enjoy the priceless treasure within you.

Our identity is not something we decide in a moment; rather, it is something we discover over time.

IDENTITY DEFINED

The first thing we need to know if we are going to discover this treasure of who we are is to know what "identity" is.

The World English dictionary defines "identity" as:

1. the state of having unique identifying characteristics held by no other person or thing
2. the individual characteristics by which a person or thing is recognized 2

It is these "unique identifying characteristics" that make us who we are. Though there are over seven billion people on the planet, there are no two people who carry the same "unique identifying characteristics". This is due to something called deoxyribonucleic acid, or as most people recognize it: DNA.

DNA is a nucleic acid that carries the genetic information in the cell. DNA consists of two long chains of nucleotides twisted into a double helix and joined by hydrogen bonds. The sequence of nucleotides determines individual hereditary characteristics. 3

The human genome has approximately three billion base pairs of DNA arranged into forty-six chromosomes. You don't have to be a scientist or mathematician to appreciate the mind-boggling number of combinations that could be made from three billion base pairs!4

Due to the incalculable variations, it would be impossible for anyone to distinguish the unique physical characteristics of every person on earth; thus, society has devised a standardized way to accurately recognize people. It is called "official identification" or ID. There are different forms of accepted ID, but most include your name, address, signature, and a photo. Due to identity theft and fraud, we are all obliged to carry our identification with us even in the simplest transactions.

A couple of years ago in mid-November my husband George and I had some pictures taken at a local department store. We had planned to use them as photo Christmas cards for our family and friends.

When we were finished the photo session, the middle aged, frumpy woman who took our pictures advised us that we should come back in about ten days to pick them up. We pre-paid for our order, thanked her, and left the store.

On his way home from the office a couple of weeks later, George stopped by the department store to pick up our photo cards. The same woman who had taken our pictures was at the counter when he arrived. He greeted her warmly, reminded her of who he was, and asked if he could see the pictures. She reached under the counter and produced a package of lovely Christmas photo-cards with George and I sitting on a bench in a snow-covered park.

George looked them over, satisfied they were what we wanted. He looked at her and said, "These are great. I'll take them."

Peering imperiously over her thick glasses, she replied, "I'm sorry sir, but I will need a piece of government-issued ID before I will release these to you."

Holding one of the pictures up next to his face and stifling a snicker, George replied, "But, ma'am, look at the picture… that's me! Isn't this proof enough that I'm the right guy?"

Pursing her lips she repeated emphatically, "No, I'm sorry sir. Our policy is not to release any pictures without official identification."

Sighing with resignation, George conceded, "Ok if that's what you require, I guess I will have to go home to get my ID."

Though we had already paid for them and George was standing right in front of the woman, holding a picture of himself that she had taken only two weeks before, she would not accept anything but official ID. Without that ID, George was unable to get what actually belonged to him.

Now, more than any time in history, identity is crucial. Not just in obtaining photos but in every area of our lives, we must know who we are and be able to defend our identity. The world will challenge you on every front; unless you're confident in your identity, you will walk away empty-handed, denied the very things that actually belong to you.

IDENTITY CONFUSION

Identity theft has been the weapon of choice used to destroy people since the dawn of time. We see the first occurrence of identity confusion in the Garden of Eden. Adam and Eve were living in a literal paradise where they reigned supreme. But one day the devil, disguised as a snake, stole everything from them through the deceptive words quoted below that caused identity confusion:

Genesis 3:5

For God knows that in the day you eat of it your eyes will be opened, and you will be like God, knowing good and evil. 5

The serpent destroyed Adam and Eve by clouding their understanding of who they were. He convinced them that they needed to eat the forbidden fruit in order to be like God. The truth was that Adam and

Eve were already like God. They were created in His very image. This is evident in the first chapter of Genesis:

Genesis 1:26-27

26 God said, "Now we will make humans, and they will be like us. We will let them rule the fish, the birds, and all other living creatures."

27 So God created humans to be like himself; he made men and women. 6

The trap that Adam and Eve fell into which cost them everything that rightfully belonged to them was a lack of understanding of who they really were. Because they didn't have a clear understanding of their identity, they were deceived into reaching for something that actually already belonged to them. They lost what they had by trying to achieve an identity they already possessed.

They lost what they had by trying to achieve an identity they already possessed.

Mankind was doomed as a result of identity theft. Fast forward a few thousand years and we see the devil trying to use the same tactic on Jesus.

Matthew Chapter 4:1-11 records the story. While Jesus was in the wilderness, Satan challenged his identity repeatedly by saying, *"If you are the Son of God…."* However, unlike Adam and Eve, Jesus knew who he was and could not be shaken in His identity. 7

Right before this temptation in the wilderness, Jesus was baptized by John the Baptist in the Jordan River:

Matthew 3:16-17

16 And when Jesus was baptized, He went up at once out of the water; and behold, the heavens were opened, and he [John] saw the Spirit of God descending like a dove and alighting on Him.

17 And behold, a voice from heaven said, This is My Son, My Beloved, in Whom I delight! 8

Satan already knew who Jesus was, but he was testing to see if Jesus knew who he was. If the devil was brazen enough to challenge Jesus' identity, then you can be sure he will challenge yours.

It's sad to say that our enemy often knows more about our true identity than we do. We are too quick to follow Adam and Eve into forgetting who we are. Too often we're chasing after things that already belong to us, and in the process we lose our sight of who we really are.

GRADUATION DISASTER

A prime example of being robbed through lack of understanding identity occurred in my grade twelve year of high school. I had met my husband when I was thirteen and he was seventeen, although we didn't start seriously dating until he was twenty and I was sixteen. Our relationship was characterized by the many ups and downs typical of young lovers. One particularly infamous moment was that of my high school graduation in June of 1982.

I attended high school in a small city in Western Canada where the graduating class was about two hundred. The graduation banquet was held at the community's largest venue, but each graduate was allowed only three guests. I had invited, as had most of the graduates, both my parents and my escort, who was George. As was customary, the escort's responsibilities for the night were to accompany me to the banquet, to escort me in the grand march, and to perform the ceremonial first dance of the evening with me.

About an hour before George was to pick me up, I was at home excitedly getting ready for the night. My older sister came into my room as I was meticulously applying my make-up and she asked how things were going. I told her how excited I was and how much I was looking forward to George being able to share the evening with me. Then she dropped a bombshell: "What do you mean, George is coming to the banquet? Don't you know that escorts don't get to eat the meal? They are only allowed to come for the ceremony."

"Oh no!" I cried in despair and confusion. "I thought that we were allowed to bring our escort to the banquet!"

"No, you're only allowed your parents. There's not enough room for all the escorts," was my sister's emphatic reply.

I knew George had rented a tuxedo and was probably on his way to pick me up. I felt terrible about having to phone him at such short notice and tell him he couldn't come to the banquet. When I spoke with him, he was understandably upset and disappointed.

All of my excitement melted away along with the make-up which ran off my tear-stained face. I got in the car with my parents and we drove in glum silence to the banquet without my beloved escort. Upon arrival however, we realized that my sister had unknowingly misinformed us. Though it had been true for her graduating class the previous year, it was not true that escorts were excluded from the banquet for this year's class. But by then it was too late to reverse the damage - George missed the banquet. When he finally arrived for the grand march, he was justifiably feeling less than happy.

What was supposed to be a night of celebration and fun turned out to be a night of confusion and pain - all because I didn't realize who I was and what belonged to me. I allowed someone else's experience to define my own and rob me of what was rightfully mine.

What have you lost through a lack of identity? Whatever it is, don't despair. You can get it back through understanding and daring to defend who you are. I love what Dr. Seuss, the author of *The Cat in The Hat,* says about this:

> *"Be who you are and say what you feel because those who mind don't matter and those who matter don't mind."* 9

At the end of your life, don't you want to say you at least lived it? Wouldn't it be a tragedy to die never having experienced all that was rightfully yours to enjoy? Discovering and enjoying your true identity is living - anything else is just a pale shadow of what your life could be. Political activist and author Anne Lamott said it so eloquently:

"Your problem is how you are going to spend this one and precious life you have been issued. Whether you're going to spend it trying to look good and creating the illusion that you have power over circumstances, or whether you are going to taste it, enjoy it and find out the truth about who you are". 10

So I ask you: How will you spend this one precious life? Will it be yours to discover who you really are - or will it belong to those who wish to shape it to fit their own design? As you continue to read this book, I believe you will be emboldened and empowered to really live your life.

2. CHAPTER TWO

COMPONENTS OF OUR IDENTITY

In the last chapter we defined identity as *"having unique identifying characteristics held by no other person or thing."* These unique identifying characteristics are not just physical. There are many facets to our identity - many characteristics that make us unique. It's important that we understand each component and its significance in making us who we are.

Components of our identity work like elements on a chemical table. Many of the same chemical elements are found in a variety of substances. However, depending on the amount of each element and their specific combinations, you can create completely different substances from the same elements.

For example, the air we breathe and the water we drink both share the common elements of Hydrogen and Oxygen, yet it is obvious that water and air are two completely distinct substances. Similarly, every person shares the same basic components of identity, but it is the respective amounts and combinations of these components that determine our absolute uniqueness.

SPIRITUAL

Of all the elements of our identity, the spiritual element is the most important. Our spirituality is like the foundation of a house. We can't see it and we can almost take it for granted, but everything rests upon it. If your foundation is not solid, then it won't be long before the whole house falls apart.

The simplest definition of spiritual identity is *your relationship with God*. Every human being on the planet has some type of a relationship with God. Some have a relationship that is very formal and ritualistic; some choose to ignore and deny the existence of God; some are even hostile towards Him; and yet there are many who share a very close and intimate friendship with Him.

Charles R. Swindoll in his book entitled *Flying Closer to the Flame* told how on April 12,1961 the first cosmonaut, Yuri Gagarin, made the first primitive little journey around the earth. He reportedly came back with his thumbs under his suspenders bragging, "I have been in the air. I have been around the earth. And I did not see God!"

The following Sunday W.A. Criswell, pastor of the First Baptist Church in Dallas, Texas made a classic statement. He said, *"Ah, if that cosmonaut had stepped out of his spacesuit, he would have seen God!" 1*

The desire to develop a relationship with God is of course a personal choice and will be unique in its experience and expression. However, the degree to which we develop this relationship is the degree to which we will have a healthy spiritual identity and a solid foundation to build our lives upon.

PHYSICAL

Our physical appearance is part of our identity. This is the part of our identity that is visible to the world. As mentioned earlier, our physical appearance is determined largely by what we inherited genetically from our parents.

If you are fortunate to be a parent, I'm sure you will agree that you never forget the sense of awe and wonder at the birth of your first child. I remember that miraculous event so clearly, even though it was over three decades ago. There I was, sweaty and exhausted after thirty hours of labour and still panting on the delivery bed, when the nurse lay this nine pound three ounce red-faced crying little creature on my belly. Though it shouldn't have been a surprise, my husband and I both looked down in utter amazement at how much he looked like us.

Every child's physical identity is something inherited from the combination of their parents' genetic codes. Yet no matter how many children a couple produces, there are never two who look exactly alike. Even identical twins, though they share many similarities, have distinguishing physical characteristics like their fingerprints, voice pattern, as well as little things like moles and freckles. Our physical identity is completely unique.

SOCIAL

Our social identity is made up of the family, culture, ethnicity, educational, and economic background we were raised in. How we relate to the world around us and how we perceive ourselves in relation to the world are greatly influenced by our social identity.

Recently I saw a heart-wrenching movie that illustrated the power of social identity called *The Good Lie. 2*

The movie is based on the true story of the mass slaughter of the Sudanese people during the late 1980s. Tens of thousands of children were orphaned and forced to wander hundreds of miles to the nearest refugee camp in Kenya. These children came to be known as the *"Lost Boys of Sudan"*.

The movie focused on a group of children whose village had been decimated and they found themselves fighting for survival as they wandered through the scorching desert in search of the refugee camp. No matter what obstacle or tragedy they faced on their perilous journey, their dedication to their family's traditions as well as their sense of loyalty and love for each other were never broken. Only five of the original seven made it to the refugee camp.

After thirteen long years in the refugee camp, four of the children, now young adults, were granted a chance for a wonderful new life in America. Elated, they boarded the plane filled with dreams of a fairy tale life. However, upon arrival it soon became apparent that the perils of the African wilderness paled in comparison to the trials that met them in this strange new land. Yet despite the collision of two completely opposing cultures, they held on to their honour, their dignity, and their true identity.

Though they found themselves in a different world, they were still the same. They interpreted their new world through the lens of their original culture. They proved the saying, *"We do not see things as they are; we see things as we are."* Social identity gives us a powerful lens through which we view the world - for good or for evil.

> *"We do not see things as they are; we see things as we are."*

PSYCHOLOGICAL

The last component of our identity is our psychological identity. It is what we will spend the majority of this book studying. Our psychological identity can be referred to as our psyche. *The American Heritage Stedman's Medical Dictionary* defines our psyche as:

"The mind functioning as the centre of thought, emotion, and behaviour and consciously or unconsciously mediating the body's responses to the social and physical environment." 3

In layman's terms, this definition states that our psyche or mind is the place where all our thoughts, feelings, and actions run through. We could say our mind is like the central hub of a railway system and our thoughts, feelings, and behaviours are the trains. All the trains are directed and run through the central hub. Our mind determines where the trains go, when they leave, and when they return. Conscious thoughts and behaviours are trains that are driven by a driver. Subconscious thoughts and actions are driven by an automated system. This automated system of the subconscious is designed by many factors which we will discuss in more detail later.

PUTTING ALL OF THE COMPONENTS TOGETHER

In this chapter we discussed the various components of our identity - spiritual, physical, social, and psychological. While each part contributes to making us who we are, some have more impact on our identity than others. To summarize and illustrate their significance and how these parts fit together, think of a car.

The physical and social parts of your identity are like the body of the car - they tell you your colour, your make, your model, and your year. Like our physical identity, this is the part of the car that is readily seen by the world around us. Some people may really like our colour and design - others may not. But in reality the body of the car is mostly aesthetic. It is not nearly as important to the function of the car as the workings that are beneath its surface.

Our spiritual identity is like the engine. The engine is one of the parts of the car that - though not readily visible - is critical to the car's functionality. The engine is built into the car by the manufacturer when it is made. Unlike an assembly line stock engine, the Creator placed a uniquely customized engine in every person when he or she was conceived. He knows better than us what we're capable of and what kind of fuel we function best on. Reading the manufacturer's manual helps us understand the purpose and potential of our car; similarly, developing a relationship with our Creator helps us understand the purpose and potential of our lives.

Another component that is beneath the surface but crucial to a healthy identity is our psyche. Our psychological identity is the gasoline that fuels the car - it's what puts the car into motion. Our psyche will determine how far we will go and how long it will take us to get there. You can have a great body and even a great engine, but without gas in the tank you're not going anywhere. And as you may well know: just any type of fuel won't work. Different vehicles require different fuels.

My husband and I learned this very painful lesson a few years ago while travelling on some back roads in an attempt to shorten a long trip. We were a couple of hours into the trip when we realized we had forgotten to fill up at the last gas station. We were driving up a long steep hill when quite suddenly we felt the car lurch violently and we were forced to pull over to the shoulder. Groaning with frustration, we started praying for someone - anyone - to find us and help us out of our desperate situation. It wasn't long till a kind farmer and his wife came by with a can of gas and told us there was an auto wrecker a few miles down the road who would be able to give us enough gas to make it home. Gratefully we drove to the auto wrecker and filled up.

Unfortunately, even though we made it home, the fuel from the auto wrecker was of such a poor quality that our engine was permanently damaged. Our psychological identity can have the same effect as gasoline. It can propel us forward, seriously slow us down, or even permanently damage us depending on its quality. Changing our thinking and our psychological identity is like changing the kind of gasoline in our tank. Poor quality gasoline will deliver poor performance in your car and poor quality thoughts will produce a poor quality of life. Conversely, high quality gasoline will produce high performance in your vehicle and a higher quality of thought will produce a higher quality of life.

That is why the remaining chapters will be dedicated to examining the health of our psychological identity. We don't want to spend the rest of our lives stalled out at the side of the road waiting to be rescued. We want to be able to drive with confidence towards our dreams.

> *"The world as we have created it is a process of our thinking. It cannot be changed without changing our thinking."*
>
> *Albert Einstein 4*

3. CHAPTER THREE

A CASE OF LOST IDENTITY

STEVEN STAYNER

It was the winter of 1972. The boisterous children poured out of Charles H. Wright Elementary School clad in sweaters and bell bottom jeans as the bell signalled the end of the day. Steven, a lively seven-year-old boy, made plans to have a game of soccer with his friends after supper and then said goodbye as he turned towards his house which was only a short distance away in the small city of Merced, California. He felt proud that he was allowed to walk home by himself on this cool December afternoon. He playfully kicked a pile of golden leaves near the sidewalk and smiled as the wind sent them swirling into the air.

As he walked he noticed a man dressed in scruffy work clothes standing on the corner handing out papers and talking with a couple of boys from his class. Curious, he began to approach them. As he drew near, the other boys began walking away, and the man turned to greet Steven with a practiced smile.

"Hi there, young man. How're you doin' today?"

"I'm good," was Steven's cheerful reply.

The man continued, "My name's Ervin, what's yours?"

"Steven," he answered.

"Steven, now that's a nice name - it's a Bible name y'know." Cocking his head to indicate the direction, he said, "I'm from the church over there and I'm looking for people to give us stuff to help the poor folk in town. Do you think your Mom'd give us anything?"

"For sure!" Steven enthusiastically replied. "My Mom's got all kinds of stuff."

Clapping his hands in delight the man exclaimed, "Great! Why don't you show me where you live so's I can talk to your Mom?"

Nodding in agreement, Steven started walking towards his house. But Ervin said that he had a friend who could give them a ride. Just then a big, white Buick sedan pulled up beside Ervin and Steven. The stout, balding driver identified himself as Kenneth and beckoned them into his waiting car. On that fateful day of December 4, 1972, little Steven Stayner accepted a sinister invitation that robbed him of his innocence, his family, and his identity.

For the next seven years Steven's kidnapper, Kenneth Parnell, subjected the boy to indescribable sexual and mental abuse. In the early stages of his abduction, Steven pleaded with Parnell to let him return to his family. However, Parnell told Steven that he had been granted legal custody of him because his parents could not afford so many children and that they did not want him anymore. Parnell changed Steven's name to Dennis Gregory Parnell. They moved from place to place in order to maintain the ruse that Parnell had fabricated, claiming that he was the boy's father. Confused, deflated, and hopeless, young Steven was compelled to relinquish his true identity and live a counterfeit one.

As the years passed, Steven's memory of who he really was faded and might have been lost altogether if not for another traumatic event. Steven's kidnapper grew dissatisfied and was no longer aroused by him as fourteen-year-old. He began actively seeking another child to gratify his depraved lust for little boys. On Valentine's Day 1980 Parnell kidnapped five-year-old Timothy James and brought him back to join the "family".

Steven was tormented as he witnessed little Timmy being subjected to the same abuse that he had endured. Unable to stand by and watch the horror unfold once again, Steven began devising an escape plan for Timmy and himself.

One night, only two weeks after Timmy's abduction, Parnell went to work at his night security job. Steven along with Timmy hitch-hiked from Parnell's remote cabin in the Yosemite forest into Ukiah, California - Timmy's home town. They tried to find Timmy's house, but after hours of unsuccessful searching, they finally went to the police.

Due to the length of time he had been with Parnell, it took several policemen some time to convince Steven that Parnell's story about his parents giving him up and not wanting him was a lie. Steven finally agreed to let the police call his family in Merced. *1*

Steven gave this statement to the police - note the incorrect spelling of his family name:

"My name is Steven Stainer. I am fourteen years of age. I don't know my true birth date, but I use April 18, 1965. I know my first name is Steven, I'm pretty sure my last is Stainer, and if I have a middle name, I don't know it." 2

The very next day Parnell was arrested and the boys were both reunited with their families. Timmy and his family were elated to be together again. Sadly for Steven, coming home to his family was not the happy reunion one might imagine. Though they were initially overjoyed to have Steven home, it soon become apparent that after living an alternate life for so long he struggled to return to his true identity. Refusing therapy, Steven's former identity was never recovered. His life ended abruptly and tragically with a motorcycle accident at the age of twenty-four.

Thankfully, not many of us have had to endure the horrific trauma of kidnapping and abuse that Steven Stayner did. However many of us still share something in common with him - a loss of identity. His loss of identity came violently through the hands of his captor. Ours usually comes through more subtle means which we will study further. But however it happens, the results of a lost identity are equally debilitating and life-altering.

HOW IDENTITY IS LOST

We can examine what happened to Steven and use that knowledge to expose a loss of identity in ourselves. There were four stages that Steven went through before his identity was irreparably damaged:

1. DECEPTION

The first stage of Steven's loss of identity began when he believed a lie. The lie was that Parnell was now his legal guardian because his parents didn't want him anymore. This lie was propagated by someone who sought to control him through deception and fear.

Many of us believe different but equally crippling lies such as these:

- "You're stupid."
- "People don't like you; they only pretend to."
- "You're so messed up, nobody will ever love you."
- "If you had been born in a rich family you could've had a good life; but you weren't, so you better just accept the fact you're never going to have anything nice."
- "Don't get your hopes up - you'll only set yourself up for disappointment."

These lies come through a host of channels. Some are malicious in their intent, but most are oblivious to the damage they've done. Usually the lies come through the means of our own poor self-image. Below is a list of some of the most prevalent avenues of identity crushers:

- Words spoken by parents, peers, and other authority figures we respect
- Judgments we've made about ourselves through comparing ourselves to others who we believe are superior to us
- Failed relationships
- Unsuccessful personal ventures and career paths

In my own life I've fought many of these lies. I got married right out of high school and entered the ministry soon after. There I was, barely twenty years old, trying to model moral and spiritual rectitude to people who were more than twice my age, who had decades of more life experiences than I. To say I felt inadequate and insecure would not even come close to describing how inept I felt.

I felt the unspoken yet rigid expectations of the people to do a host of things I was ill-equipped to do, like playing the piano and leading the music department. When I confessed I had no skill to do these tasks, the leaders of the church were aghast.

In addition to the music department I was expected to oversee all the women's activities which included everything from baby showers to overseas missions projects, visiting the sick and downcast, and to teach Sunday School and Bible study. Of course all these duties were expected without financial remuneration. It was just what a "good pastor's wife" did.

My response to this immense pressure was to believe the lie that I was not a good person unless I kept everyone happy and performed to their expectations. Consequently, I learned to play the piano and lead the choir. I studied the Bible so I could teach; I organized all kinds of showers, conferences, and missions projects. And above all, I learned to never expect money for the countless hours I spent serving the people. After all "the love of money was the root of all evil" and I certainly didn't want people to think I was evil.

However, after years of working to gain people's approval, despair and resentment started to take root within me. I was angry and felt trapped into being this "person" who people applauded, while the real me was slowly but surely dying. I felt I had no expression for who I really was and that I was in grave danger of losing my true self altogether.

Finally, after about twenty years of striving for approval, I arrived at a place of complete exhaustion. I was actually close to a nervous breakdown. I realized that if I didn't stand up for myself, nobody else would. I had to speak and act for the real me. I made some tough decisions that cost me dearly in the public approval ratings, but set me on a new path of self-discovery and freedom that I am still on.

I have remained in ministry but have redefined the way I do it in accordance to who I believe I am and where my strengths lie. I no longer lead the music department, children's ministry or organize missions projects. Instead I have trained other people to do these tasks so that I can pursue my passion for teaching, writing and counselling people. I have established boundaries with my time and have learned the magical little word, "No." In addition, once I came to see myself and my contributions as valuable I soon moved past feeling guilty for receiving financial compensation for my work. Hopefully, as I share candidly about the lies that once kept me from being my authentic self, you will be able to avoid some of the mistakes I've made.

Just one of these lies is enough to confuse you and cause you to lose confidence in yourself. Unfortunately, like myself, you are probably not dealing with one isolated attack, but rather multiple, repetitive assaults on your identity. If an aggressive counter-attack is not launched, then you will come to believe the lies you have been bombarded with and will eventually forfeit your true personhood.

Of course, the biggest problem with deception is that you don't know you're there. If you did, you would no longer be deceived. Steven didn't know that what he believed wasn't true. The circumstances seemed to support what Parnell was saying. After all, his parents never called or tried to find him. From Steven's perspective the lie seemed true. Though his parents were desperately searching and praying for his return, Steven's warped perception became his reality.

So it is with the lies we believe about ourselves. Our perception becomes our reality. The circumstances in our lives can seem to support the lie's validity. For instance, if you are fired, immediately negative thoughts begin assaulting your mind. You believe the lie that because you were fired you won't get a good reference and you'll never get another job. Because you believe you are stuck professionally, you become discouraged and disgruntled. Over time your negative attitude becomes apparent to everyone - including those who may have previously considered promoting you. Your belief about yourself becomes a self-fulfilling prophecy. Now your perception has actually defined your reality. The lie is now truth to you.

While it is true that you lost your job, it is not true that your professional life is over because of it. Failing does not make you a failure. As the saying goes: *"You may have done what they said you did, but you are not who they say you are."*

> *Failing does not make you a failure.*

Thomas Edison refused to believe he was a failure just because he failed. After struggling for months and months to develop a viable electric light bulb, Edison was interviewed by a young reporter who boldly asked Mr. Edison if he felt like a failure and if he thought he should just give up at this point. Perplexed, Edison replied, "Young man, why would I feel like a failure? And why would I ever give up? I now know definitively over 9,000 ways that an electric light bulb will not work. Success is almost in my grasp." Shortly after that, and after over 10,000 attempts, Edison invented the light bulb. Edison refused to believe that he couldn't succeed just because he had experienced failure - lots of failure! 3

Failure can actually be the catalyst to success as seen in the life of Steve Jobs, the former computer guru and co-founder of Apple Inc. Jobs helped to design, develop, and market some very successful lines of personal computers in the early years of the company including the Apple II series and the Macintosh. Although he was fired from Apple in 1985 after a power struggle with the company's board of directors, he refused to believe the lie that past failure excluded future success. By 1998, he was once again CEO of Apple and eventually brought the company to unprecedented world prominence and profitability. 4

What would have freed Steven Stayner from the web of deception in which Parnell had bound him? Someone who told him the truth. As a seven-year-old boy he was not able to see through the lies and extricate himself from the prison he was in. He needed outside intervention. Sadly none came.

Think of this book as an outside intervention into your situation. Whatever lies you have believed about your lack of ability; your lack of intelligence; your failure to develop intimate lasting relationships; or the hopelessness of your financial situation, see these things for what they are - lies. They have no power over you unless you believe them. This book can be the passageway to freedom from the lies which have imprisoned you.

2. REJECTION

The second stage in identity loss is a feeling of rejection. Once Steven believed the lie that his parents no longer loved or wanted him he soon felt the pain of their rejection. Parental rejection has far-reaching effects in a child's life. Ronald Rohner of the University of Connecticut, co-author of the new study in *Personality and Social Psychology Review* had this to say on the subject:

"In our half-century of international research, we've not found any other class of experience that has as strong and consistent effect on personality and personality development as does the experience of rejection, especially by parents in childhood. Children and adults everywhere - regardless of differences in race, culture, and gender - tend to respond in exactly the same way when they perceived themselves to be rejected by their caregivers and other attachment figures."

Rohner found that in response to rejection by their parents, children tend to feel more anxious and insecure, as well as more hostile and aggressive toward others. The pain of rejection - especially when it occurs over a period of time in childhood -- tends to linger into adulthood, making it more difficult for adults who were rejected as children to form secure and trusting relationships with their intimate partners.

Moreover, Rohner says that emerging evidence from the past decade of research in psychology and neuroscience is revealing that the same parts of the brain are activated when people feel rejected as are activated when they experience physical pain. He said, *"Unlike physical pain, however, people can psychologically re-live the emotional pain of rejection over and over for years." 5, 6*

Rejection is something we all experience at some level. We humans are hard-wired to *"belong"*, and so it hurts when we feel excluded. In our efforts to escape the pain of rejection we often trade a portion of our true selves and adopt a false persona that we believe will be more acceptable to those we want to maintain relationships with. This can be demonstrated by stifling our convictions on a controversial social issue rather than risking the reproach of offering a different opinion. It could be in choosing a career - we opt for a more *"acceptable"* occupation rather than risk the rejection of choosing to follow our artistic side. In whatever measure we trade our true selves for a false self will be the measure to which we relinquish our true identity.

The pain of rejection is something that can cripple us, just as it crippled Steven, unless we make a conscious choice to move past it. A popular axiom states: *"It's not what happens to you but how you respond to what happens to you that determines success or failure."*

> *In whatever measure we trade our true selves for a false self will be the measure to which we relinquish our true identity.*

Harvard lawyer turned visionary career catalyst, Tama Kieves, was quoted as saying:

"I know that when a door closes, it can feel like all doors are closing. A rejection can feel like everyone will reject us. But a closed door leads to clarity. It's really an arrow… we will go somewhere else." 7

Abraham Lincoln learned through a great deal of pain not to let rejection stop him from following his dreams. Though many doors were closed to him, he kept going until the one he wanted finally opened.

At age seven Abraham Lincoln's family was forced out of their home and he had to work to help support the family. He was only nine when his mother died. Due to the unfortunate situation, he only received one year of formal education. The rest of his extensive learning came through his own avid reading and self-discipline. However, when he applied to law school he was rejected.

Two of his business ventures failed, he was fired from his job, he endured the shame of bankruptcy, he lost eight different elections, he suffered from clinical depression, and he had a complete nervous breakdown before becoming president in 1860.

Lincoln had no control over the rejection he suffered and neither do we. We can't control the people or circumstances in our lives that seem to be against us. It's impossible to avoid rejection and the pain that accompanies it. But it is possible to learn how to deal with it. Instead of being controlled by it, we can learn to use it to our advantage. According to a contemporary Japanese writer Haruki Murakami, *"Pain is inevitable but suffering is optional." 8*

Sylvester Stallone is another individual who suffered a lot of rejection before getting his *"big break"*. He lived every day with one consuming dream - to become an actor. All he needed was a part to play, but no parts were offered to him. Undaunted, his dream drew him to write his own part.

He put together a script and began looking for someone to produce it. He went from agent to agent, studio to studio, but no matter what he did, nothing came of it. He was rejected countless times. Even if he had given up, most would still have called him courageous for how long he kept going in spite of all the rejection. But that's not where the story ends.

Finally, somebody liked his script. The timing couldn't have been better as he was flat broke. Yet because his dream to be an actor was so great, he turned down the $330,000 he was finally offered for his script as the producer wanted someone else to play his part.

Even though he was barely able to feed his family, he kept searching until he got exactly what he wanted. He eventually starred in the movie he wrote and won an Oscar. It was then followed by five sequels. For holding onto his dream and turning down the buyout offer, he has received several million dollars per picture and his films have grossed nearly a billion dollars. What would have happened if Sylvester Stallone had given up because of repeated rejection? Nobody would have ever known who Rocky was or been inspired by his courage. 9

Stallone had this to say about rejection:

> *"I take rejection as someone blowing a bugle in my ear to wake me up and get going, rather than retreat."* 10

I hope these true life stories serve as a wakeup call. If you've suffered rejection, and I think it's safe to say we all have, don't allow it to make you retreat into self-pity. It's time to get off the defensive. It's time to move into the offensive position - take back your identity and live the life you were born to live.

3. HOPELESSNESS

The third stage of identity loss is a sense of hopelessness. As the days turned to weeks and the weeks turned to years, Steven Stayner gradually gave up hope that he would ever live the life he desired - back with his real family. Once hope was relinquished he lost any reason to fight for his identity.

In the battle to maintain our identity there are times when darkness seems to swallow all our dreams and the only thing left to validate their existence is hope. There are many things in life that, like Steven's abductor, can extinguish our hopes - divorce, illness, bankruptcy, job loss, infertility, death of a loved one, and the list can go on. The only thing that can bring light to these dark places is hope.

Desmond Tutu rose to prominence at a very dark time in the history of South Africa. In the 1980s he became a spokesman against apartheid in that nation. In this heroic battle he often faced what looked like overwhelming opposition and yet he said:

"Hope is being able to see that there is light despite all of the darkness." 11

Though we may not have control over the darkness, the longer we choose to sit passively in the black of hopelessness, the harder it will be to turn on the light of hope. This phenomenon is seen in certain aquatic life which live deep near the sea floor where no sunlight ever reaches them. These blind creatures actually avoid sunlight and are doomed to feed on the dead refuse that slowly falls to them from the creatures who live in the light above.

There are countless people who choose to live in a similarly dismal place - subsisting only on the cast-offs of others and wandering the perpetual night of hopelessness. The easiest way to identity them is by their catch phrase: *"Don't get your hopes up - That way you won't be disappointed."* In closing the door to hope, they unwittingly close the door to new opportunities, new relationships, new ideas, and a new life.

Without hope you are not living in the brilliance of your true identity; you are merely existing as a shadow of who you could be. Living your true identity takes courage - courage to face the darkness and the things that compel you to accept a lesser version of yourself. Refuse to allow hopelessness to rule you.

> *"Let your hopes, not your hurts, shape your future." 12*
>
> *Robert H. Schuller*

4. COMPROMISE

The fourth and final stage in identity loss is compromise. This is complete once deception, rejection, and hopelessness have strangled the individual to the extent that they actually adopt the distorted identity as their own. Steven Stayner was compelled to be the person his captor desired for over seven years. Eventually he learned that submission and compromise won him at least a measure of acceptance and approval.

Though Steven never completely lost awareness of who he really was, he chose not to give opportunity or expression to his true self. Over the years he became *"comfortable"* in this compromised identity and became more alienated from his true self. It wasn't until little Timmy came that Steven's dormant identity was finally awakened enough to see himself as he truly was - a victim of identity theft - which armed him with sufficient motivation to change his situation.

Many of us don't realize how much of ourselves that we have lost or compromised until a critical moment in our lives. Crisis has a way of ripping back the curtains and exposing all the lies with one blinding flash of reality.

It never ceases to amaze me, when counselling couples in crisis, to hear that one partner had no idea the other was so unhappy. They are oblivious until they see the partner pack their suitcase and head for the door. Suddenly the crisis shines light on a problem that had existed for months or even years in the shadows of denial.

Whatever crisis you face now or in the future, don't run from it; welcome it as an opportunity to align yourself with your true identity. The events that led you to this point of pain may largely have been out of your control, but the worst thing you can do is to compromise your true self in order to avoid the crisis.

Dr. James B. Richards in his book *How to Stop the Pain* had this to say about compromising our true selves:

"Our personal development is stifled when we are controlled by what others think. However, the control that others wield over us is imaginary. It is not empowered by their intention; it is determined by our beliefs. No one

can take control of us - we give it away. We give our control in exchange for something else. There is something we feel we can gain, something we value more than having control of our lives. When we value something more than freedom, we will surrender our control of self... Anytime we give away our freedom, anytime we feel controlled, we should look to ourselves instead of looking to others and accusing them. We should ask ourselves, 'What do I value in this situation so strongly that I am giving up control of my life?'... Make no mistake, anywhere we feel controlled, we have exchanged our freedom for something that we consider to be more valuable." 13

In other words, we must take responsibility for our own identity. There is far too much emphasis in our society today on assigning blame rather than taking action towards positive change. It has rightly been said that it serves no purpose to shout at the darkness; we must turn on the light.

If we feel stifled or controlled, then we must take the action necessary to take back control. Once we identify that we have forfeited our true selves in order to avoid rejection we need to muster our courage and do whatever it takes to regain the part of ourselves we've lost. This will involve confrontation, establishing boundaries, and in some cases discontinuing a relationship. But as unpleasant as this may sound, if we ever hope to enjoy our authentic selves we must do it.

Being authentic is a challenge in any walk of life, but particularly in the music industry. To be successful in this profession one faces a tremendous ongoing battle to be true to yourself and not just perform for producers and audiences. Toby Keith and Janis Joplin - two very successful artists - shared some simple yet profound words about protecting your true self:

"Don't compromise even if it hurts to be yourself." 14

Toby Keith

"Don't compromise yourself. You are all you've got." 15

Janis Joplin

To echo these words, never give up the fight for authenticity. Challenge the lies. Rise above the rejection. Never give up hope. Refuse to compromise who you are. Be yourself - everyone else is already taken.

> *Be yourself - everyone else is already taken.*

4. CHAPTER FOUR

WHAT DO YOU SEE INSIDE?

"What lies behind us and lies before us are small matters compared to what lies within us."

Ralph Waldo Emerson 1

Our psychological identity simply defined is how we see ourselves. It is what we see when we look inside ourselves. Our psychological identity will ultimately determine the quality of life we enjoy.

Author David Eckman defined psychological identity as:

"... the instinctive picture of ourselves that we carry around inside of us." 2

It is what we believe ourselves to be. It is what we project to the world.

This instinctive picture is like your passport. Your passport must include a clear picture of you. I remember going to a local vendor to get my passport photo taken a few years ago. I had dressed up and carefully done my hair and make-up, complete with shiny lip gloss. I felt quite confident in my appearance until the photographer asked me to fold down my collar, shove my hair unflatteringly behind my ears, and to wipe all the nice shiny lip gloss off - they didn't want the glare ruining the clarity of the picture. I was going for a glamour shot and they were going for a reality shot. What a lot of humbling work for a simple snapshot.

However, if you've ever gone through the process of getting a passport you know that a clear accurate picture is essential. Without that clear picture you will never get your passport and you will never be able to travel outside your country of origin.

Without knowing your identity or having a clear inner picture of who you are - you will never travel outside your place of origin emotionally, socially, psychologically, or spiritually. For many people, being stuck in their current psychological state evokes as much hopelessness as the thought of being trapped in a war torn, impoverished nation without a passport.

Our identity, according to Eckman, is not something we logically decide to adopt. It is something we acquire non-rationally as a product of our family and cultural background. Our identity is instinctive and emotional in nature. He said:

"As a vulnerable child grows - and every child is vulnerable, it will adopt as its own, the picture of itself that its family and environment hands to it. This will occur not as a rational act but as an intuitive acceptance of reality. That is why a flagrantly false identity can have such power. Having irrational emotional power, the picture is accepted by a child's mind during the vulnerable growing-up years. That picture will become the foundation of the identity of the later years." 3

This principle of adopting a false identity is illustrated in the story I told in the Introduction about my feelings of rejection when I discovered my baby book in the attic. The fact that my parents may have wished for a boy and may have even struggled to come up with a name for me didn't necessarily mean they rejected me. It was my perception of the events that caused me to feel rejected. It was a non-rational emotional picture born out of my vulnerability as a child. However, this perception became my reality. I consequently interpreted every interaction with my parents through the lens of rejection.

For example, when I was about nine years old I was helping my dad to clean out the family car. As I was vacuuming under the front seat I found a dime and was so excited. I told my dad that I was going to put it in my piggy bank, expecting him to praise me for being so lucky and resourceful. Instead, he berated me for being so miserly and selfish as to keep the money for myself.

Now, I can see through the adult lens of rationality and be able to recognize that my dad was struggling to provide for his family and was over-reacting because of it. However, at the time his words and tone served to deepen the wound of rejection in my vulnerable childhood ego.

Children who grow up in environments that lack nurturing will often develop a performance mentality. Because their care-givers didn't display affection readily, the child learns that in order to gain approval they must do something that pleases them. The parents probably never uttered the words *"You must earn my love,"* but the child learns this instinctively and non-rationally. He receives the emotional reward of their approval when he performs successfully and thereby establishes a foundation for his life based on a flawed perception of himself.

AN ELEPHANT NEVER FORGETS

It has been said that an elephant never forgets. In 1999 the keeper of the Elephant Sanctuary in Tennessee witnessed firsthand the amazing powers of recall that pachyderms possess.

Jenny, an adult female elephant, had been a resident of the sanctuary for a number of years when a new elephant named Shirley was introduced to the herd. The two elephants became so animated and excited it seemed like their meeting was an emotional reunion of two old friends. They were bellowing and checking each other over with their trunks for what seemed like familiar scars.

The zoo keeper knew that Jenny had performed with the travelling Carson & Barnes Circus before coming to the sanctuary, but she wasn't familiar with Shirley's history. After doing a little research she discovered that Shirley had in fact been in the same circus with Jenny for a few months - twenty-three years earlier. *4*

Elephant trainers, called mahouts, use this knowledge of the elephant's memory to their advantage when training these giant mammals. *5*

A young elephant, still wild, is tied to a wooden frame or between two tree trunks where he is unable to move. And it is then, while tearing at the ropes and flailing with his trunk, that he is introduced to his mahout. In order to be broken in, the young elephant is repeatedly jabbed with an elephant hook and beaten. At the same time, the mahout talks to him in a calming voice.

Fear, pain, thirst, and hunger finally make the elephant relinquish all resistance. When the elephant begins to accept its fate, the mahouts allow it to take a bath in a river and to eat, although it continues to be tied to a working elephant throughout. *6*

After a few weeks, the young elephant will be tame enough to be led, still shackled and supervised by several mahouts, but no longer accompanied by working elephants.

After this "initiation phase", the elephant starts its proper training to become a working elephant.

Through this cruel conditioning the young elephant is trained to believe that he cannot prevail against the mahout. Even when he grows to his full and massive size of seven-and-a-half tons and can carry up to almost twenty-thousand pounds, the African male elephant lives the entirety of his seventy years in complete submission to his mahout, tragically unaware of his true strength. *7*

Life can often inflict the same kind of cruel conditioning upon young tender souls. When we are young we are not psychologically prepared to resist the emotional attacks and the subsequent wounds that debilitate us. We grow up like the young elephant in fear and pain till we lose sight of our true identity and accept this servile condition as our lot in life.

But this is not who we really are. We, like the elephant, only need to be awakened to our true ability and strength in order to exercise it. The power the mahout holds over the elephant is only in his mind. Similarly, there is no person, no lack of education, no prejudice, no financial restriction, and no physical disability that can stop you unless you believe it can.

I grew up believing that there were the "haves" who enjoyed a charmed life. They got all the good breaks, they were born with silver spoons in their mouths, and they enjoyed all the best that life had to offer.

Related to this belief, I also believed there were the "have-nots" of which group I was a lifetime member. In this group you never caught any breaks because the odds were always stacked against you in favour of the "haves". Us "have-nots" were doomed to eke out a meagre existence that was marked by poverty, anonymity, and misery.

Till I was thirteen years old, I lived in a rundown trailer court on the edge of town. The trailer I grew up in was only eight feet wide and twenty feet long. There were no bedrooms or doors separating rooms - just beds suspended on the wall. We didn't have a room to play in so my dad built a lean-to room and a porch on the side of the trailer. He worked hard to provide for us and we never went hungry, but we were definitely in the "have-not" category. We wore clothes purchased at church rummage sales, grew most of our food in the garden, and rode old dented bicycles that my mom spray-painted.

Fast-forward a few years - I was nineteen and married only one year when George and I were offered the opportunity to purchase our first home. We didn't have the money for a down payment, but the people who owned the house offered us a rent-to-purchase agreement. What a huge break for us "have-nots!" We were thrilled with the thought of actually owning a house but a little apprehensive about getting a mortgage and being in debt.

I thought I should ask my dad for some financial advice before we signed any documents. The words he spoke, though I'm sure he meant to encourage me, stabbed my heart like a knife: "Why would you be worried about debt? You'll be in debt for the rest of your life." It was as if I had received a financial death sentence that would psychologically imprison me for years. My father's ominous words seemed to be coming to pass as my husband and I struggled to stretch our meagre salaries from paycheque to paycheque. There were times we even had to roll the coins from our kids' piggy banks just to buy milk for them.

But thankfully, my husband and I came across some people who challenged our poverty mindset. We began to hear things like, *"Never let your past dictate your future," "Let your test become your testimony," "Your attitude determines your altitude,"* and many other radical ideas that began to open our minds to the possibility that we could move out of being the "have-nots" and actually become members of the "haves". This revelation continues to be a life-long journey of self-discovery that has truly revolutionized my identity in not only the financial realm but in every facet of my existence.

Bob Gass said, *"It's not what you go through in life that messes you up; it's what you keep going back to!" 8*

> *"It's not what you go through in life that messes you up; it's what you keep going back to!" 8*

In other words, you may have come from a background of familial dysfunction, mental illness, substance abuse, divorce, or any number of identity challenging events. But these events cannot stop you from becoming who you desire to be unless you continue to revisit them in your mind. You may have failed at some things, but that does not make you a failure.

Moving to a new place in your mind is no easy task. American author and poet Richelle E. Goodrich accurately described the intense, sustained effort that is required to re-invent yourself:

"You will find there are times you must grasp your life with both hands and forcefully steer it in a new direction and then strain to hold your course until the storms of fear, weakness, and doubt abate." 9

So make a decision today to not go back to those places of pain and defeat in your mind. In essence you will be replacing that old picture of yourself with a new one. You need to understand, however, that it's not as easy as copying and pasting an image from the internet onto a prepared document.

It's more like scrubbing a lifetime of ugly, profane graffiti off the walls of your mind, sandblasting the grime and mildew that's accumulated from all the years of exposure to the elements, carefully selecting what you want to paint on your fresh clean walls, and then applying the brush strokes lovingly one by one, day after day, year after year, till you see the masterpiece you imagined your life could be.

David is one of Michelangelo's most famous works, and has become one of the most recognizable statues in the entire world of art. Standing thirteen-and-a-half feet tall, the double life-sized *David* is depicted patiently waiting for battle, prepped with slingshot in one hand and stone in the other.

The marble block used by Michelangelo was originally excavated for a statue to be carved by another sculptor in 1464, but the block was not fully carved. When Michelangelo received his commission in 1501, he was presented with the challenge of using the block which had already been worked upon to some degree. He had to work with what he was given. *10*

There's not one of us who is a completely untouched block of marble. We all must learn to work with what we've been given to create what we desire. We have to see the beauty in the block in order to carve it out.

So what do you see when you look inside yourself? Do you see beauty or repulsiveness, unique potential or latent inadequacy, success or failure? Be sure of this one truth: whatever you look for you will find. Decide right now to see that amazing work of art within you and have the courage and determination to carve it out.

5. CHAPTER FIVE

A CASE OF MISTAKEN IDENTITY - UNMASKING FALSE IDENTITY

> *"The privilege of a lifetime is to become who you truly are."* 1
>
> *Carl Gustav Jung*

Before DNA testing became part of the judicial process, prosecution lawyers relied heavily on eye-witnesses to convict people of their alleged crimes. Unfortunately, eye-witness accounts were not always accurate and many innocent people suffered for crimes they did not commit. Poor lighting, poor eyesight, or distorted memories all can contribute to making a false identification. According to statistics, over seventy-five percent of the cases of DNA exonerations have involved mistaken eyewitness identification. 2

One case that demonstrates mistaken identity is the case of Ronald Cotton. In 1984, Jennifer Thompson was raped. During the attack, she studied the attacker's face, determined to identify him if she survived the attack. When presented with a photo lineup, she identified Cotton as her attacker. Twice, she testified against him, even after seeing Bobby Poole, the man who boasted to fellow inmates that he had committed the crime for which Cotton was convicted. After Cotton served ten-and-a-half years of his sentence, DNA testing conclusively proved that Poole was indeed the rapist. 3

Thankfully such tragic cases of people mistaking our identity are not an everyday occurrence. Unfortunately it is all too common that we get our own identity confused. How could it be possible to not recognize yourself? When we believe that who we are is not acceptable, we will adopt an identity that we believe *will* be acceptable. If we persist in this long enough we won't be able to recognize or identify our true selves.

Brené Brown is an American author and research professor at the University of Houston Graduate College of Social Work. She explains in her book *Daring Greatly* how the acceptance we crave from others threatens our authenticity and can never be satisfied till we learn to accept ourselves as we are. She said:

"Because true belonging only happens when we present our authentic, imperfect selves to the world, our sense of belonging can never be greater than our level of self-acceptance." 4

I can confirm this principle from my own experience. I grew up as the ugly duckling in my family. My sister had thick wavy hair that naturally fell into lovely ringlets; I, on the other hand, had scraggly thin hair that refused to do anything besides lay flat against my head. My sister was slim; I was "chubby". I often came home from school crying because kids teased me and called me fat. Over the years I came to believe that if I wanted to be accepted I needed to be pretty, and being slim was the most important part of being pretty.

At the age of twelve I made a decision to radically cut down my food intake and to implement a strict exercise regime. The results were swift and dramatic, as were the resulting compliments I began to receive. This strengthened my resolve to continue losing weight and my belief that this new identity as a slim, beautiful person was the only way I could achieve happiness and acceptance.

Unfortunately, no matter how much weight I lost, the internal picture I had of myself remained overweight and repulsive. Even when I weighed ninety pounds I still saw myself as obese and grotesque. I envisioned the real me to be a hideously fat person lurking inside my emaciated body that might at any moment escape captivity and expose me as the fraud I believed I was. I lived in constant fear that the blimp on the inside of me was going to break out and take over the body that I worked incessantly to keep under control.

My eating disorder controlled my life for almost fifteen years. After years of trying to be the person I believed would make me and other people happy, something happened that was like a tiny flicker of light in the dark world of my twisted identity.

My mom forced me to see a doctor because I had ceased menstruating for about nine months and all her efforts to make me eat had failed. When the doctor assessed me he told me that secondary amenorrhoea often occurred in women who were held in prisoner of war camps. Once the body fat ratio reaches a critical deficiency, the body will begin to shut down. It suddenly dawned on me that I was voluntarily and literally starving myself to death.

This event was the beginning of my realization that I no longer knew who the real Sandra was and the person I was trying to be was making me miserable. It was then that I began the long road back to self-recovery.

Drs. Hal and Sidra Stone describe the issue of discovering your identity in their book, *Embracing Your Inner Critic*. They described how a false identity is projected in two ways:

a. *"The primary self"* is the person you want the world to see. This is the person you believe will be accepted. In my case, the skinny girl was my primary self. Skinny Sandra was the person I wanted others to see in order to gain the world's approval and acceptance.

b. *"The disowned self"* is the person you don't want anyone to see. This is the person you believe will be rejected. My disowned self was the fat girl. I lived in constant, agonizing fear that fat Sandra might be discovered and sentenced to a life of ridicule and rejection. I longed to rid myself of this fat phantom that I believed lurked within me. 5

Neither of these identities represented the real me. They were fabrications I created to ensure my acceptance. Somewhere hidden under these false identities lay the real Sandra - bound, gagged, and denied any expression.

You may be reading this and have come to a foggy or possibly acute awareness that you have been living with a false identity. Up till now you may have considered it your "game face" or the persona you have grown accustomed to adopting when you're with people. You may have believed this was just part of who you are.

If you are just coming to this place of self-awareness and are recognizing that you have been living out of a false identity, consider this a timely wake up call. The scary fact is that if you continue to live out of a false identity long enough, you will come to believe that this is who you are. You will lose touch with your true identity, otherwise called your *"authentic self"*.

Psychology teaches that we will reject any part of our personality that we believe doesn't fit the person we are trying to be. Thom Rutledge in his book *The Self-Forgiveness Handbook* explains how damaging it is to reject our true selves:

"... learning self-forgiveness is the classic human search for identity. As long as we remain in hiding from the so-called negative aspects of ourselves, we remain incapable of embracing all of who we are. When we consider only certain of our human characteristics acceptable, we have no choice but to remain fragmented, experiencing ourselves as less than whole. And since rejecting certain aspects of ourselves does not exorcise them from our personalities, we find ourselves in a stagnant pool of guilt (for having such

unsavoury traits) that left alone, will become at least the toxins of self-distrust and dislike, and possibly the poisons of self-disgust and hatred." 6

Rutledge aptly describes the psychological torment that we often endure because of a lack of self-acceptance. In our efforts to live up to people's expectations and our own self-imposed standards, we lose sight of our authentic selves.

Alex grew up in a home where hard work was the measure of a person's worth and laziness was despised. He prided himself on being industrious and struggled to allow himself to simply relax. He always felt vaguely guilty for indulging in an extended period of inactivity. If he wasn't doing something all the time, he could feel anxiety starting to build as his inner critic hissed words of condemnation and shame into his subconscious mind.

Susan grew up in a matriarchal home in which her mother prided herself on being able to "do it all" - pursue a successful career, as well as be a good mother and wife. Susan became a successful corporate finance executive and married a very supportive and caring husband named Mark. Her work was demanding and she often felt exhausted after a hard day. But instead of asking for help from Mark, who would have been happy to help, she felt compelled to prepare a home-cooked dinner and keep on top of all the domestic duties that a "good wife" should tend to.

One particularly trying day she came home early with a splitting headache, popped a couple of Advil, and flopped on the couch for a much needed nap before Mark came home. Within moments she drifted into a dead sleep till she heard him coming through the door. Panic-stricken that he might see her napping instead of working, she bolted from the couch and straightened her hair, terrified that Mark might consider her a slacker.

Let me give all of you work-a-holic, performance-driven folks like me a news flash: There is nothing wrong with taking a rest when you need it. Truthfully, your spouse would probably be happy you stole a nap if it meant they didn't have to endure your grumpiness the rest of the evening.

A false identity and the somewhat bizarre and irrational behaviour that accompanies it does not develop overnight. Behaviours and belief systems are painted onto the canvas of our inner self-portrait over a lifetime with the brush of conditional love. When we perceive that love must be earned, we will adopt almost any behaviour in order to receive it.

We would do well to heed the advice of Andrew Matthews:

> *"A healthy self-love means we have no compulsion to justify to ourselves or others why we take vacations, why we sleep late, why we buy new shoes, why we spoil ourselves from time to time. We feel comfortable doing things which add quality and beauty to life."* 7

Dr. David Hawkins in his book *Dealing with the CrazyMakers in Your Life* shares a story about how this process of gradually disconnecting from your true identity transpires:

"A seven-year-old comes home from school, discouraged because she wasn't invited to her friend's birthday party. Her mother says, 'Oh, it doesn't really matter. She's just being selfish. You didn't want to be her friend anyway.'

How is that child going to develop? Her mother's statement invalidated her perceptions, and her declaration that this rejection didn't matter was the exact opposite of the truth. The mother presented the experience to the girl backward. Can you imagine what the girl might have been thinking and perhaps what she would have liked to say had she been older and more mature?

'Mother, you're wrong. It does really matter. Yes, my friend is being selfish, but I do want to be her friend.'

Sadly this child will probably learn to disconnect from her true feelings and identity. Her world will take on an increasingly distorted, abnormal shape. If her mother doesn't change, this little girl will learn to distrust or stifle what she sees, thereby altering her sensate function; ignore what she thinks, thereby denying her thinking function; limit her hunches or intuitive function; and repress her emotions or feeling function.

Consider what happens when this child's experience is repeated many times over while growing up and then again as an adult. What happens to this child as she grows into adulthood and perhaps marries an aggressor who continues the process of telling her what to think and do?

...Just as in her childhood, her thoughts, feelings and perceptions are invalidated and distorted but this time by an angry, aggressive husband. She gradually learns she must disconnect herself from her sensate awareness that something is wrong. She must disconnect from her feeling awareness, or she will become discouraged and depressed. She must disconnect from her intuitive awareness or she will realize that she is in danger. She must disconnect from her thinking awareness, she must not reason too much, or she will be told she is not making sense. Someone else, in this case her husband, now has the power to take away her freedom. With this abuse occurring repeatedly, he has the power to redefine her inner reality (or identity)." 8

As a counsellor I have spent countless hours trying to help people just like the girl in this story to regain their authentic selves. The first step to regaining their true identity is always unmasking the false identity.

James Douglas "Jim" Morrison was an American singer, songwriter, and poet best remembered as the lead singer of *The Doors* - a rock band from the late sixties. Despite his Bohemian lifestyle Jim had great insight into our compulsion for hiding our true selves and was quoted as saying:

"That's what real love amounts to - letting a person be what he really is. Most people love you for who you pretend to be. To keep their love, you keep pretending - performing. You get to love your pretence. It's true, we're locked in an image, an act - and the sad thing is, people get so used to their image, they grow attached to their masks. They love their chains. They forget all about who they really are. And if you try to remind them, they hate you for it, they feel like you're trying to steal their most precious possession." 9

It's time to rip off our masks and live authentically. We have only one brief life. What a tragedy it would be if we should pass through without ever having truly lived it.

6. CHAPTER 6

CAN I TRUST MYSELF?

As a counsellor I often get asked questions like, *"Can I trust myself? Is what I'm feeling right? Should I follow my heart?"* These questions are not easily answered, and the answer is not the same for every person. We need to examine where our thoughts and feelings are coming from before we make a choice to act on them.

Remember how in Chapter Two we used a car to illustrate the parts of our identity which all fit together to make us an individual? I want to use the car analogy again, but in a different way. I want to use it to reveal what is actually driving your life.

THE STEERING WHEEL

A car is meant for motion. There are many things that contribute to the motion of the car, but the most important one is the steering wheel. Without the ability to steer a moving car, any movement would soon end in disaster.

So it is in our lives. We too are meant for motion. But just as we must keep a firm hold on our car's steering wheel, so we must also keep a good grip on our life's steering wheel. The steering wheel of our lives is something we all use on a daily basis. Sometimes we use it to steer our lives into wonderful places filled with love, creativity, and happiness. At other times we use it recklessly and crash into all manner of pain and destruction. What is this steering wheel of our lives? It is none other than our mouths.

What we say sets the direction of our lives. We cannot afford to allow self-defeating talk out of our mouths any more than we would carelessly let go of or suddenly yank a car's steering wheel while driving top speed down the highway. Both scenarios would be disastrous.

Though the steering wheel is not what actually powers the car, it is what directs the power. The power of the car actually comes from its engine and the steering wheel is what we use to direct that power. Similarly, our mouths are not our engines, but what we say directs the power of our engines. Our engines are our identity. As we stated earlier, identity is: *"the instinctive picture of ourselves that we carry around inside of us"*. *"What's in the well, comes out the bucket"* is not just a cliché - it is a profound truth. What we think about ourselves is eventually revealed through our words and in our behaviour.

This principle of identity-directed speech is outlined in the Bible in Luke 6:45

"... .What you say flows from what is in your heart." 1

In his new book *Beyond the Power of Your Subconscious Mind,* author C. James Jensen vividly describes how the way we talk about ourselves shapes our lives:

This internal thinking, or self talk, occurs through the conscious area of our mind. What most people are unaware of is our self talk becomes instructions to our subconscious, whose duty is to carry out the "orders" given to it by the conscious area of our mind. The subconscious is our own personal servo-mechanism that works on our behalf twenty-four hours a day, seven days a week.

How does it work? Imagine an ocean liner crossing the sea, with the captain of the ship barking out commands to the crew. The crew, however, is located in the hold of the ship, below the water line, unable to see where the ship is going. The captain is the conscious area to the mind. In this example, the crew is like the subconscious.

So when the captain commands to the crew, "Full speed ahead, 15 degrees to the North," the crew simply responds, "Aye-aye, sir" and carries out its orders precisely. The crew does not care if it runs the ship into the rocks, collides with another vessel, or gets the ship safely to its destination. It is totally non-judgmental and does not question "the boss."

This is a powerful metaphor of the relationship between the conscious and subconscious areas of the mind. These are not two separate minds, but rather, two spheres of the same mind.

So, what we say to ourselves or how we may describe ourselves to others occurs through the conscious level of thought. If we are repeatedly saying...

- *"I can't do this."*
- *"My marriage is falling apart."*
- *"I never seem to have enough money."*

...then these become "instructions" to the subconscious, whose duty it is to work tirelessly to ensure these "instructions" are brought into reality. It doesn't question whether these are "good" or "bad" instructions (for us). It simply carries out what we have instructed it to do. 2

Neuroscientist Dr. Caroline Leaf has devoted her life to studying the human brain and how thoughts impact our lives. In her book entitled *Switch on Your Brain* she shows through documented research how thoughts affect our words, our behaviours, our bodies, and even our DNA.

We may have a fixed set of genes in our chromosomes, but which of those genes are active and how they are active has a great deal to do with how we think and process our experiences. Our thoughts produce words and behaviours, which in turn stimulate more thinking and choices that build more thoughts in an endless cycle.

...research shows that DNA actually changes shape according to our thoughts. As you think those negative thoughts about the future - the week ahead, what a person might say or do, even in the absence of concrete stimulus - that toxic thinking will change your brain wiring in a negative direction and throw your mind and body into stress.

According to Dr. Herbert Benson, MD, president of Harvard Medical School's Mind-Body Institute, negative thinking leads to stress, which affects our body's natural healing capacity. Toxic thinking wears down the brain.

The Institute of HeartMath, an internationally recognized non-profit research organization that helps people reduce stress, discusses an experiment titled 'Local and Nonlocal Effects of Coherent Heart Frequencies on Conformational Changes of DNA.' This study showed that thinking and feeling anger, fear, and frustration caused DNA to change shape by tightening up and becoming shorter, switching off many DNA codes, which reduced quality expression.

So we feel shut down by negative emotions and our body feels this too. But here's the great part: the negative shutdown or poor quality of the DNA codes was reversed by feelings of love, joy, appreciation, and gratitude. The researchers also found that HIV positive patients who had positive thoughts and feelings had 300,000 times more resistance to the disease than those without positive feelings. 3

Our words produced by our thoughts are the by-product of our identity. What we say about ourselves exposes what we believe about ourselves. It's not just what we say to other people that can derail us; more often it is what we say to ourselves that gets us in a wreck.

Contrary to popular belief, everybody talks to themselves - it's not the exclusive, secret habit of neurotic people. Talking to yourself is normal - talking to yourself in a derogatory way is not. Negative self-talk is one of the most deadly, self-destructive habits you can develop.

Maddy Malhotra, an inspiring self-esteem expert, self-help author, and international motivational speaker grew up in poverty in India. He borrowed eight thousand dollars and moved to the UK, determined to change his lot in life. He wanted to prove the naysayers wrong and become a man of worth.

He encountered many obstacles along the way that threatened to destroy his dream, including his limited command of the English language as well as his lack of money and connections. But these obstacles were not the things that ultimately determined his success or failure. He said that it was his self-talk that propelled him to a new life. 4 According to Maddy:

> *"The most influential and frequent voice you hear is your inner-voice. It can work in your favour or against you, depending on what you listen to and act upon."* 5

Professional Life Coach Malti Bhojwani claims in her book entitled *Don't Think of a Blue Ball* that what we believe and speak about ourselves actually has a tangible impact on our lives. She writes:

> *"Our stories become self-fulfilling; we will always live up to the story. So make it a desired one."* 6

THE ENGINE LIGHT

In addition to the steering wheel, there is another small, seemingly insignificant mechanism that is critical to safely driving your car. It is a little red indicator called the engine light. The engine light is located on the dashboard and will flash when your engine is running low on oil.

Imagine a sunny but crisp October afternoon. You've decided to take a drive through the country to take in the glory of the autumn colours before the impending wind strips the gold and crimson leaves from their branches. A few minutes into your expedition, however, you notice the engine light beginning to flash.

"Oh no! Not now!" you grumble to yourself. Next you begin to reason in your mind, "I just got started and if I don't see the leaves today they will all be gone by tomorrow. I'm sure if I just go a little farther everything will be fine."

So onward you go - up the hills and through the valleys bedecked in all the glorious splendour only autumn can provide. Lost in the reverie, you forget about the little red blinking light till suddenly your car begins to lurch violently. As you impulsively pull over to the shoulder, you see thick grey smoke billowing from under the hood.

Our emotions are the engine light that begins to flash when something is out of order. While we cannot "steer" our lives with our emotions, we cannot ignore their warning. If we choose to ignore our emotions and keep driving, we will soon find ourselves on the shoulder of life with smoke billowing from every part of our lives.

Emotions that drive us are not always easily identified. They can be a subtle yet destructive force eroding the very fabric of our existence. Such was the case with Harold. His marriage had failed because of an affair that he had with another woman. To his ex-wife's credit she remained on friendly terms with him even after the divorce and they shared all the family birthdays and holidays together amiably.

Despite the forgiveness that Harold had been granted by his ex-wife, he could not forgive himself. The guilt and shame he carried drove him to workaholism and frequent fits of rage. Harold would readily acknowledge his negative behaviour, but was unable to relinquish the guilt and shame that were causing it. Deep down he believed he deserved to be punished for his *"sin"* and therefore denied himself absolution.

Eric grew up in an alcoholic, abusive home. His mother was divorced and frequently brought drunken men home after a night at the bar. Violence generally ensued upon their arrival, and the local police and child protection services were a common part of the weekend's chaotic activities. Young Eric did his best to hide his tumultuous home life from his friends at school, but lived in constant fear they would find out how dysfunctional his life and family were. He believed the only way to survive was to stifle the pain and put on a good front. In his mind, exposure meant rejection.

Though Eric is now a successful businessman, the shame of his past still subconsciously haunts him. It fuels his compulsive need to accumulate wealth and his excessive need to feel respected. In moments when he feels threatened financially or relationally, he will react with fits of anger which invariably subside to bouts of depression.

In these and many other similar cases, it is obvious that ignoring our emotions can lead to lifelong neurosis.

Dr. William Frey, a highly respected biochemist, led a research team that studied tears for fifteen years. They discovered that tears shed for emotional reasons are made up of different chemicals than tears that are caused by irritants or by peeling onions. The emotional tears contain toxins from the body that onion-generated tears do not contain.

They concluded that chemicals that accumulate in the body during times of stress are removed from the body inside tears of sadness. Not only that, but they contain high quantities of a hormone that is one of the best indicators of stress. Suppressing those tears actually contributes to physical diseases that are aggravated by stress, including high blood pressure, heart problems, and peptic ulcers.

And did you know that only humans can weep? All animals produce tears to lubricate their eyes, but only people cry because they are upset or sad. 7

We need to stop and figure out what's causing our emotions to overheat. Emotions are not the problem any more than the little red light on the dash is the problem. They are only an indicator of the real problem under the hood.

Sigmund Freud claimed that:

"Unexpressed emotions will never die. They are buried alive and will come forth later in uglier ways." 8

In my experience as a counsellor, I've found that one of the biggest reasons people bury their emotions is that they believe that having negative emotions is bad. *"Good people don't have bad feelings"* is the false assumption that riddles them with guilt and reluctance to express their emotions.

Coupled with this erroneous belief of denying negative emotion is the equally destructive supposition that it's wrong to have needs. However the truth is that when our basic needs for unconditional love, acceptance, and security are not met we are going to have a negative emotional reaction.

However, as we cultivate a healthy perception of ourselves, we will begin to feel more comfortable articulating our needs and expressing negative emotions that arise. We will gain an understanding that having a negative emotion does not mean you are a negative person. A healthy self-perception will produce a healthy self-expression.

The root that's triggering our emotions often goes deeper than we think. Our emotions come from our thoughts and our thoughts come from what we believe about ourselves - that inner picture of ourselves that we talked about earlier. Our identity is ultimately at the crux of most emotional problems.

African-American playwright August Wilson faced many obstacles on his way to winning a Pulitzer Prize. Growing up in a home of poverty and divorce as well as enduring relentless racial prejudice would have made it easy for him to live below his potential. In spite of everything, Wilson learned to overcome life's challenges and come to self-actualization. He advocated:

"Confront the dark parts of yourself, and work to banish them with illumination and forgiveness. Your willingness to wrestle with your demons will cause your angels to sing." 9

So to answer the question at the beginning of this chapter: *"Can I trust myself and what I'm feeling?"* I would like to share what Dr. James B. Richards has to say about self-awareness:

"If I am hurting and in pain, it is doubtful that I can see clearly enough to get to the real root of my problem. That would be like allowing a mentally

disturbed patient to evaluate and diagnose his own problems. The treatment would be no better than the diagnosis. When we self-diagnose, the self-prescribed treatment is often the source of additional pain." 10

This does not mean we will never overcome our personal struggles. What it does mean is that we must be committed to a process of growth in order to properly address these deep-rooted issues. In addition we should seek the counsel and support of a qualified and objective individual who can help us identify our blind spots.

The more we move away from our false identities and embrace our true selves, the more we will be able to trust our own perceptions about ourselves and the challenges we face. Knowing who we are will not remove every bump in the road, but it will give us the ability to navigate successfully through them.

7. CHAPTER SEVEN

CLEARING OUR VISION

WHO CUT THE CHEESE?

We've all heard the saying, "Seeing is believing". But is that really a true axiom? Just because we see something with our eyes does not guarantee we correctly interpret what we are looking at.

A few years ago when my husband and I directed a private college, we took a group of students on a trip to the Maritimes. During our time there, we visited a unique tourist attraction called Magnetic Hill, located near Moncton, NB . The attraction boasted that gravity was reversed on their site. Upon arrival, we were told to drive our vehicle to the bottom of the hill, put the engine in neutral, and enjoy the ride up the hill. To our wonder and amazement the van did roll up the hill at a steady pace without any assistance from the driver. Our eyes told us that gravity had indeed been reversed, but our minds knew it was merely an optical illusion. Seeing is not always a credible path to believing.

The truth is, we don't see things as *they* are - we see things as *we* are. We all view the world through the lens of our own experiences and beliefs. This is so important to remember when we are trying to establish a clear sense of who we really are. We cannot always trust our own perceptions. A blog posted in October of 2014 contained this simple but profound statement:

> *"The eyes are useless when the mind is blind."* 1

This principle is illustrated by a comic story. Sam locked the door of his condo, jumped excitedly into his Jeep loaded with gear, and headed down the road. He was meeting four of his buddies at the lake for their annual guys only fishing weekend.

He had the farthest distance to drive, so by the time he got there his friends already had a fire blazing and dinner on the table. He was famished and ate ravenously. After the long drive and the big meal, it wasn't long before his eyelids began to get heavy and he dozed off in the warmth of the fire.

About an hour later he was awakened by the boisterous racket of his friends as they sat around the poker table. He began to rouse himself, intending to join the fun. But suddenly he became acutely aware of a horrible smell.

Sam called over to his friends at the table, "Do you guys smell that?"

Snickering slightly they replied, "What smell?"

"Don't tell me you can't smell that! It's rancid! It's like something died in here." Sam declared.

"Hey, he who smelt it - dealt it!" laughed one of his friends.

"No seriously! I think we should look around the cabin to see if a mouse is rotting in a trap or something."

"Go ahead if you want. We're in the middle of a game," was the chortled response.

Determined to uncover the origin of the repugnant odour, Sam began his search in the kitchen - first the fridge, then all the cupboards, and of course the garbage - all to no avail. Next it was the bathroom, then both bedrooms - still no offending culprit was found.

Frustrated now, he walked outside to get some fresh air and clear his head. But to his surprise and dismay, he found the lecherous odour was there too. He hollered back into the cabin, "You guys, that stench is everywhere. This whole place is contaminated. We need to get out of here before the toxic fumes kill us."

Unable to contain themselves any longer, his friends burst into uncontrollable laughter. Finally one of them got enough composure to wheeze out the truth: They had smeared Limburger cheese under his nose while he was sleeping.

While Sam had spent hours fruitlessly trying to ascribe blame to an outside source, the putrid smell was all the while emanating from right under his nose. He promptly boxed them all on the head and washed the offensive substance off his face - recognizing at last the true source of his vexation - himself.

As funny as this story is, it holds a sobering truth. The great majority of the "foul" things in our lives are not due to outside sources - they originate from within our own minds. I am not negating the fact that life often hits us with tragedy, disappointment, betrayal, and pain. We have no way of stopping people from smearing Limburger cheese on us, but we can stop the cheese from remaining there and poisoning our entire lives.

Just because you had an abusive relationship with a man doesn't mean all men are abusive. Just because you made a bad investment doesn't mean you need to live in fear of every financial opportunity or think that all brokers are crooks. Just because you struggled in school doesn't mean you're incapable of learning and developing to your full potential. Remember in Chapter One that Abraham Lincoln only had one year of formal education.

It is these kinds of flawed mentalities that keep people locked in prisons of fear, bitterness, and prejudice. One event or experience cannot ruin your life or steal your identity unless you believe it can. Storms can rage all around you but they have no power to harm you unless you allow them to rage inside you.

Storms can rage all around you but they have no power to harm you unless you allow them to rage inside you.

NARROW-MINDED MADNESS

Dr. James B. Richards in his book *How to Stop the Pain* explains how our mindset determines how we see ourselves and our relationship to the rest of the world:

"When people pass a judgment or develop strong opinions, they lock themselves into selective processing. Studies show that forming strong opinions causes activity in the reticular activating system, which is located at the base of the skull. This neurological activity produces a mental state in which one can see only what he or she has predetermined. In other words, you no longer see it how it is. Your mind selectively processes information that confirms your perception while ignoring data that is contrary to your point of view. We all have done this. We all have looked at a label and were sure that it said one thing, only to later discover that it said something completely different.

"The mind seeks equilibrium. It seeks to validate your opinions. Once you make a judgment about a person, whether good or bad, you will notice only what validates your judgment. You will interpret all the person's actions on the basis of that judgement…" 2

I have fallen prey to getting locked into misguided perceptions many times. One occasion that is vivid in my memory happened about twenty years ago while my husband and I were the pastors of a small church in rural Saskatchewan.

The women of the church had devised a program called "Secret Sisters" to encourage friendship and networking among the women. We had a tea party and each participant drew a name from a hat that they kept confidential. That name was the person they were to become a "Secret Sister" to. The women were encouraged to pray for their Sister and send anonymous notes and small gifts on her birthday and other special occasions. At the end of the year we had a party to reveal who our "Secret Sisters" were.

The program took off immediately and many of the women looked forward to receiving the anonymous notes of encouragement and the little gifts. My "Secret Sister" was exceptionally thoughtful - never missing an occasion to express her kindness and love for me.

During the course of that same year, one of our staff members became disgruntled and though we tried to accommodate his concerns, he eventually decided to leave and find employment elsewhere. In my mind, this of course meant that his wife must have become disgruntled too. Though she had not spoken to me directly on the matter of them leaving, I believed because of my past experience in similar situations that if he was offended she would be too.

In anticipation of her impending rejection, I began to distance myself from her emotionally. It wasn't long before I began to notice that she wasn't as friendly as usual and that she seemed to be avoiding me. Then one day, unexpectedly and only weeks before they were to move, she called and asked me to go for lunch with her.

I thought to myself, "Uh-oh! Here comes the confrontation. She waited till the very end to tell me how mad she was and how disappointed she was in me." When I met her at the restaurant, I steeled myself for the moment, put on a practiced smile, and sat down across the table from her, nervously waiting for the inevitable showdown.

To my utter amazement and reproach she did nothing of the sort. She told me she wanted to get together because they were leaving before the "Secret Sisters" would be revealed and she wanted to let me know how much she had enjoyed being my "Secret Sister". She told me how she felt her love for me had grown through the experience and hoped mine had too.

My interpretation of her avoiding me or being not as friendly as usual were simply fabrications of my own fearful perceptions. I was not seeing things as they were, but as I was. When I'm not clear in my own self-perception, I can never hope to be clear in my perception of others. The only thing I did right through that entirely humbling process was to keep my mouth shut. Thankfully I didn't speak hurtful words out of my insecurity that potentially could have destroyed a beautiful friendship. She was never aware of the mental gymnastics I had been putting myself through because of seeing things through my narrow judgment.

> *When I'm not clear in my own self-perception, I can never hope to be clear in my perception of others.*

PACHYDERM PERSPECTIVE

C.S. Lewis once said:

"What you see and what you hear depends a great deal on where you are standing. It also depends on what sort of person you are." 3

This truth is illustrated so vividly in the story of when Billy and his two pals Jimmy and Tommy went to the circus. They ran all the way from their neighbourhood to the outskirts of town where Barnum and Bailey's Travelling Circus had pitched their tent. Hundreds of people were lined up outside waiting to see the main attraction - the elephant show.

The boys took their place at the back of the long line that shuffled slowly forward while the spectators filed to their seats. When the boys finally reached the entrance of the tent, the ring-master who had been directing people to their seats approached them and announced rather brusquely, "The tent is full. No one else will be allowed in."

Completely shocked and deflated, the three boys choked back their tears and began trudging dejectedly back home. Suddenly Billy had an idea: "Why don't we sneak around to the back of the tent where the elephants are waiting before they go into the ring? We can peek in and nobody will even see us!"

Jimmy and Tommy agreed and they darted back to the rear of the big top. As they drew near they could hear the ring master announcing that the elephants were next in line for the show ring.

"Hurry up you guys!" whispered Billy fiercely. "Find a hole in the tent somewhere so you can peek in and see the elephants before they go inside!"

Scampering as quickly and silently as they could, all three boys soon found a peephole to steal a glimpse of the giant mammals before they shuffled away. They stared in wonder at the marvellous creatures for a brief moment, then stole silently away so as not to attract attention and met at the edge of the fairgrounds to share their adventure with one another.

Breathless with excitement, Billy said, "Did you see that elephant? He looked like a long skinny snake."

"What are you talking about?" Jimmy asked incredulously. "That's not what he looked like at all! He looked like a great big tree trunk."

Tommy argued that they were both out to lunch, insisting instead that the elephant had giant leathery wings. The boys argued all the way home, each one convinced of what they saw and determined to prove the others wrong.

In reality they had each seen the same elephant from a different position. Billy saw the tail; Jimmy saw the legs; and Tommy saw the ears. Because they were so sure of what they had seen, they refused to look through another hole in the tent or view the other person's opinion worthy of consideration.

When you are confronted with a person who has opposing core values, a conflict is inevitable. The way you see the world is from a completely different position. Neither of you are *wrong* in your perception. But both of you are *limited* in your perception.

We must remind ourselves: How I see it is not how it is, it is just how I see it. Nevertheless, my perception ultimately becomes my reality. As our perceptions form our reality, they form our identity - how we perceive ourselves in relation to the people and the world around us. That inner picture of ourselves is based on our perception of self.

> *"We'll believe a lie that we've heard all of our life before we'll believe the truth that we've only heard once."*
>
> *Unknown*

The mind seeks to organize the information it receives. Therefore it will automatically reject information that doesn't fit into our "peephole". Our minds will only allow us to see things from a different viewpoint if we are willing to let go of our preconceived ideas. We have to look through someone else's peephole to understand a new perspective.

SUPER-WOMAN

Carol was what most of her friends called "Super-woman". She excelled at everything she undertook: she had a successful career, a loving family, and an immaculate house. She was adept at building, sewing, landscaping, and could even drive heavy machinery. She hosted large dinner parties regularly, always serving delicious new gourmet fare. In spite of her busy schedule, she always had time for a friend in need and always made sure she followed her rigorous exercise regime.

Though her friends admired her beyond measure, Carol never gave herself credit for all her accomplishments. She constantly downplayed herself and her abilities. Though her accomplishments were self-evident, Carol's mind continually rejected the accolades of her friends and held tightly to her self-effacing image of herself.

Dr. Richards in his book *Escape from Co-Dependent Christianity* has this to say about our self-perceptions:

"Whatever we choose to hold in our thoughts is what we choose to experience. What we experience is what determines the way we relate to the world around us." 4

Are you ready to experience better things in your life? Would you like to see yourself in a more positive light? Then it's time to look through a new peephole. The peephole is really your thoughts. Whatever thoughts you allow to enter your mind will shape your identity and determine the quality of your life.

Bestselling author Joyce Meyer echoes the necessity for changing your thoughts in order to change your life:

"Negative thoughts are fuel for discouragement, depression and many other unpleasant emotions. We can't have a positive life and a negative mind. Our thoughts - our focus - is what determines where we end up." 5

We can't have a positive life and a negative mind.

In order to see your full and true identity you will have to be willing to shift your mental position. Be willing to consider that your current opinion of yourself is not the full picture. Seek to discover a new vision of yourself. Allow yourself the opportunity to explore new ideas, relationships, and adventures.

"You're always with yourself, so you might as well enjoy the company." 6

Diane Von Furstenber

8. CHAPTER EIGHT

REMEMBER WHO YOU ARE REDISCOVERING TRUE IDENTITY

We can easily see how our identity can be lost through dysfunctional families, broken or abusive relationships, and a myriad of other negative factors. But how do we re-discover our true identity once it's lost? How do we get that accurate clear and positive picture of ourselves inside our consciousness?

In June of 1994, the animated movie called *The Lion King* took centre stage and became the biggest box office smash of the year. The film later went on to become the highest-grossing hand-drawn film in history, the highest-grossing 2D animated film in the United States, and the 20th-highest-grossing feature film of all time. *1*

The movie has universal appeal and illustrates the tragedy of a lost identity as well as the triumph of regaining it. Simba was the impetuous yet adoring son of Mufasa, the lion king of the Pride Lands. Simba was thrilled by the fact that one day his father's vast kingdom would be his. He was born to be a king - that was his place "in the circle of life", or we might say that was his identity.

But true to life, there were those who worked to thwart his identity. Scar, who was Simba's murderous uncle, deceived him into believing that Simba was the cause of his father's untimely death. Full of shame, fear, and confusion, Simba fled to a place far away from his home, his friends and family, and his identity.

Years later, Nala, his childhood sweetheart, found Simba living a purposeless life of self-indulgence. She curtly reminded him of who he really was and challenged him to return to the Pride Lands and assume his responsibilities and his rightful place as king. Simba, still filled with deep-rooted shame, refused and stormed off into the jungle only to encounter Rafiki, the Pride Lands' mandrill shaman.

Rafiki told him that his father, Mufasa, was still alive and led Simba to a pond where he was visited by the ghost of his father who spoke the immortal words, *"Remember who you are!"* Simba finally realized that it was time to face the shame and pain and to take his rightful place as king of the Pride Lands.

Upon Simba's return and the ensuing battle against Scar, Simba learned the truth that his father's death had come by the hands of Scar. Empowered by the truth, he was finally and completely restored to his true identity.

Though *The Lion King* is just a Disney animation, there are four significant lessons we can learn from Simba about re-discovering our true identity:

1. He listened to people who saw him in his true identity.

2. He took responsibility for where he was at.

3. He faced his fears.

4. He fought to regain his true identity.

If we find ourselves in an identity crisis like Simba and truly desire to live out our full potential, then we can't just remain passive. We need to actively employ these four simple principles which we will discuss at length in this chapter.

1. LISTEN TO PEOPLE WHO SEE YOU IN YOUR TRUE IDENTITY.

> *"A true friend never gets in your way unless you happen to be going down."* 2
>
> *Arnold H. Glasow*

The first lesson in regaining a lost identity sounds simple - just listen. But if you have ever been frustrated in your efforts to communicate with another person, you know that listening is sometimes a difficult concept. Just because someone hears what you say doesn't necessarily mean that they understand or welcome what you are saying. True listening involves not just hearing words but grasping the importance of those words, embracing their meaning, and adjusting behaviour accordingly.

For instance, you may hear your friend tell you, "You're awesome!" However, if you don't believe that you are awesome, you will block the compliment mentally. As you subconsciously reject what you hear, you will render yourself incapable of really "listening" to and embracing what your friend is saying. *We need to be aware that every time we reject a compliment we are rejecting the best part of ourselves by denying its existence.*

Simba had Nala his childhood friend, Rafiki the shaman, and even the apparition of his father who recognized his true potential. But it still took Nala's angry disappointment, Rafiki's repeated knocking on his head, and the stern words of his father to awaken his slumbering identity. He had repressed all his dreams of being a king and was reluctant to embrace them again.

If people who love you keep seeing something in you that you don't, maybe it's time to actually listen to them. Maybe, just for a moment, you need to look at yourself through their eyes. Very often people who love us are less critical of us than we are of ourselves.

If we actually spoke to other people the way we speak to ourselves we would likely have no friends willing to bear the verbal abuse. Negative self-talk is one of the most self-destructive weapons that we wield. Nothing will undermine your potential for living your true identity like negative self-talk.

Another reason we need to listen to people who see us in our true identity is that they are not emotionally attached to the false identity we are carrying. Simba had become comfortable with his false self by developing friends and adapting his behaviour according to his new identity. He had to be willing to give up these cozy, familiar relationships and behaviours that defined him in his present existence.

When we actually "hear" what others are saying and we recognize how far we have fallen from our true selves, we need to be willing to walk away from relationships with those who don't see our true potential. We must qualify those who enter our inner circle of friendship by whether they see us as we currently are or as we can be. People who are close to us should be those who challenge, inspire, and bring out our best.

If we truly want to live to our full potential, we need to listen to people who love us - people who see who we really are.

"Wounds from a sincere friend are better than many kisses from an enemy." 3

Proverbs 27:6

"A true friend is someone who thinks that you are a good egg even though he knows that you are slightly cracked." 4

Bernard Meltzer

2. TAKE RESPONSIBILITY FOR WHERE YOU ARE AT.

> *There may be many good reasons why you are where you are, but there are no excuses to stay there.*

Once Simba discovered that his Uncle Scar was to blame for killing his father and deceiving him into abdicating his rightful place on the throne, he had a life-altering decision to make. He could remain a victim of his past or he could choose to be the master of his present and architect of his future. He wisely chose the latter, realizing that though his uncle was the cause of his loss of identity, it was he himself who had the power to recover what had been lost. His uncle had no control over him now unless he relinquished it through fear and self-pity.

Taking responsibility is the second key in recovering from a false identity. Except in cases of victimization such as abuse and violent crimes, we have to be willing to acknowledge that we are what we are today largely because of choices we have made. Just as in Simba's case with his uncle, there may have been people and forces arrayed against us, but we still must accept the responsibility for our part in shaping our lives. Though we can sometimes legitimately blame other people and situations for our loss of identity, assigning blame won't fix the problem. We need to dig through the ashes, and accept the responsibility for rebuilding our lives.

Not that many years ago I learned a lesson in taking responsibility. I had come to a place of discontent and frustration in my life. I looked at other people my age who seemed to be so much farther ahead financially than I was. I have to confess I was envious and feeling a bit sorry for myself.

But then it dawned on me that I was in the financial situation I was because of the choices I had made: I chose to get married before I went to college; I chose to have kids and stay at home with them; I chose to volunteer my time in ministry. I had to take responsibility for my choices and the results of them.

Once I accepted responsibility for my choices, I quit feeling sorry for myself. I began to make new choices: choices that moved me in the direction of my dreams. I realized nobody could make those choices for me, nor could they stand in my way once I had made them. As a result of taking responsibility, the frustration and self-pity left me and instead I was filled with a sense of empowerment and excitement that I was actually in a place to become what I believed I could be.

We cannot change the past. Though we might wish to, we cannot rewind the tape and edit the pain from our lives. But we can make a choice to not allow the pain to define us. Tragically people often label themselves and identify themselves by their past pain.

For instance, you might be someone whose marriage failed, and you might identify yourself by saying, "I am divorced." While it is true you went through a divorce, that is not who you are. Don't allow yourself to be labeled. You are a valuable individual with a tremendous opportunity to explore who you really are without the encumbrance of a debilitating relationship.

I once read a comic story that illustrates how maintaining a victim mentality and refusing to take responsibility is counterproductive to building a strong identity:

A man was walking down the beach one day when a seagull flew overhead and pooped on his nose. He became so angry at the seagull. He reasoned within himself, "That seagull did this to me and he's going to have to come back and get this off of me!"

When he returned to his friends they were all repulsed. "What is that smell? Stay away from me!" they all shouted. Then they ran away from him. He became even more angry at the seagull: "Look what you've done to me," the man cried. "You come back right now and get this off of me."

When he went home that night, he wanted to be intimate with his wife. But she immediately kicked him out of bed and demanded that he go wash his face. He lay on the couch, lonely and dejected, contemplating how the seagull was ruining his life. His friends had run away from him, his wife had rejected him, and he hadn't done anything. All he could think was, "It's not my fault!"

When he went to work the next day, people quickly moved to the other side of the room to avoid him. The odour had become unbearable. The man had stopped bathing, because if he bathed, he might remove the poop from his nose, which would mean that the seagull would have gotten away with his unfair treatment.

Finally his boss called him in and said, "None of the clients want to do business with you. None of the coworkers can stand to be in the same room with you. Either you wash that poop off your nose, or you're fired." The man's response was, "How unfair can you get? Why are you all persecuting me? I didn't do anything. I didn't put this on my nose. I shouldn't be the one to have to wash it off."

So now he sits alone under an overpass, victimized by the world. And every day he looks out at the sky, because he knows who is to blame. And one day that rotten seagull will have to come and clean up his nose.

Though the story is exaggerated, we must constantly be on guard against the temptation to assign blame rather than take responsibility for our lives. John F. Kennedy once said:

"Let us not seek to fix the blame for the past. Let us accept our own responsibility for the future." 5

> *"There are two primary choices in life: to accept conditions as they exist, or accept the responsibility for changing them."* 6
>
> *Denis Waitley*

Simply the fact that you are reading this book tells me that you are someone who has chosen to take responsibility for your life. Be encouraged - you are already ahead of ninety percent of the rest of the population who would rather complain about their lives than do what it takes to change it.

3. FACE YOUR FEARS.

The third principle in recovering a lost identity is to face your fears.

Simba had established a false identity based on a fear of revealing his true identity. How could he be the king after he had been responsible for his father's death? His whole life had been spent running from his past mistakes which he believed disqualified him from future success.

If people actually knew what he had done and what a scoundrel he really was, he feared that nobody would accept him. He believed his only chance for acceptance was to hide the crimes committed by this loathsome self he was so desperate to conceal. Simba had to overcome his shame and fear of failure in order to be the leader that he was born to be.

According to inspirational writer Bob Gass,

"Only when you consider your failure to be final, are you finally a failure. Failure is not an event, only an opinion, and as long as it's not your opinion you can come back and succeed." 7

"Failure is not an event, only an opinion, and as long as it's not your opinion you can come back and succeed." 7

It takes emotional courage to embrace your true identity. We often worry: "People might reject me if they knew what I really thought or how I really felt." While it may be true that not everyone will understand or accept you in your true identity, when you have the courage to embrace your true self, you will finally be free from the torment and limitations of your fears. You will never know what's on the other side of your fears till you have the courage to push past them.

Just because we face our fear doesn't mean we will never feel fear. Fear is a natural response to things that we perceive as threatening. However, even if we feel fear, we ultimately have the power to choose not to let it control our lives. Courageous people feel fear as much as everyone else, but they choose to push past their fear and do it anyway.

Nelson Mandela learned through suffering years of racial prejudice and imprisonment that overcoming fear and having courage was absolutely essential to fulfilling his dream of freeing the people of South Africa. He stated:

> *"I learned that courage was not the absence of fear, but the triumph over it. The brave man is not he who does not feel afraid, but he who conquers that fear."* 8

Popular American poet and lecturer Ralph Waldo Emerson faced a lot of opposition from his contemporaries towards his new and unconventional ideas which included abolitionism. He had to battle self-doubt and fear as he sought to bring about change to the mid-nineteenth century's philosophical community during the volatile years of the American Civil War. He had this to say about facing fear:

"Whatever you do, you need courage. Whatever course you decide upon, there is always someone to tell you that you are wrong. There are always difficulties arising that tempt you to believe your critics are right. To map out a course of action and follow it to an end requires some of the same courage that a soldier needs. Peace has its victories, but it takes brave men and women to win them." 9

We must learn not to run from our fears but to embrace them. We need to see fear as a friend rather than an enemy. Fear can be the catalyst that forces us to rise from our current limitations and to step into the expansive passion of our truest and best selves.

Often one of the best ways to help you face your fear and recover your true identity is to simply ask yourself the question, "What am I so afraid of?" Instead of expending all your energy running, use it to fuel your courage to stop, turn around, and look your fear squarely in the face.

What do you see? Is it a fear of rejection? When you're running, that fear seems ominous as it shouts out threats like, "If you don't conform you're not going to have any friends. Your reputation will be ruined. People will think you're foolish." And on and on fear will taunt you till you stand up to it and say:

"My true friends will love and respect me more for being true to myself. Why would I want to keep relationships with people who will only accept me if I do what makes them happy? Life is too short - It's time I do what makes me happy!"

Often our fears are much more terrifying in our imaginations than in reality. Researchers have found that 92% of the things we worry about never come to pass. That 92% is comprised of 40% that never happen, 30% that are in the past and we can't change, 12% that are other people's affairs which aren't even our business, 10% is over sickness, leaving only 8% of our fears which are even likely to happen. *10*

There was once a village where the children were told, "Whatever you do, don't go near the top of the mountain. It's where the monster lives." One day, some brave young men decided they wanted to see the monster and defeat it. Halfway up the mountain, they encountered a huge roar and a terrible stench. Half the men ran down the mountain screaming. The other half of the group got farther up the mountain and noticed the monster was smaller than they had expected - but it continued to roar and emit such a stench that all but one man ran away. As he took another step forward, the monster shrank to the size of a man. The man took another step and it shrank again. It was still hideously ugly and it stank, but the man could actually pick it up and hold it in the palm of his hand. He said to the monster, "Who are you?" In a tiny, high pitched voice, the monster squeaked, "My name is Fear." *11*

If you have the courage to face your fears, then you will find one day that the things that frightened you the most were really nothing at all.

Eleanor Roosevelt once said:

"You gain strength, courage, and confidence by every experience in which you really stop to look fear in the face. You are able to say to yourself, 'I lived through this horror. I can take the next thing that comes along.'" 12

4. YOU MUST FIGHT TO REGAIN YOUR TRUE IDENTITY.

Simba had to fight a life and death battle in order to re-establish himself in his true identity. If he lost this battle he would never achieve his true potential nor his rightful place. His Uncle Scar and those aligned with him were not about to just step aside so he could assume the throne, even though they knew it was his birthright.

Make no mistake: you will have to fight a mortal battle if you decide to regain your true identity. Your true life hangs in the balance. There will be people and circumstances that will resist your decision. It would be naive to believe that everyone will celebrate the recovery of your true identity. Some would prefer that you serve their dreams instead of your own. They are happy with things as they are. Change can threaten people because they don't know how or if they will fit into this new reality you are creating.

Years ago I worked as a receptionist in a medical office. This was for the most part a pleasant job with the exception of one particularly difficult co-worker who happened to be my supervisor. Initially she seemed cordial and helpful, but with time the doctors began to see potential in me and gave me some of "her" duties. Threatened by the increasing favour I was receiving and the skills I was developing, her controlling nature suddenly came to the forefront and made working with her almost intolerable.

I knew I had to confront her and establish boundaries in our relationship if I was ever going to grow. Her intimidation was not just affecting me in my professional life - it began to creep into my personal life. I often left the office crying because of her foul moods and stinging criticism. When I finally gathered enough courage to tell her that I would not tolerate her ill-humoured behaviour, she surprisingly didn't have much to say. It seemed as if she were stunned that I would speak so tersely to her.

However, she fought back in other ways. She became sullen, irritable, and even insidiously vindictive. I had to continue to fight to hold the ground I had won in the initial confrontation as she tried to covertly turn the other staff against me and refused to assist me in tasks that were previously shared. Eventually I was promoted to be the head of a different department and was thankfully no longer under her supervision.

In the end I learned a valuable life lesson: If I don't fight to define my own identity - somebody else will define it for me.

If I don't fight to define my own identity - somebody else will define it for me.

You may find yourself in a situation or relationship where you feel controlled and are hesitant to confront for fear of losing your position or relationship, but let me encourage you with the words of *New York Times* bestselling author Joyce Meyer:

"You can buy friends and acceptance by letting people control you, but you will have to keep them the same way you obtained them. It becomes very draining after a time, and you will end up resenting them for the very thing you allowed them to do. I have come to believe that if I can never say no to a person in order to remain in relationship with him or her, then that is probably a relationship that I don't need." 13

I have come to believe that if I can never say no to a person in order to remain in relationship with him or her, then that is probably a relationship that I don't need." 13

A few years ago I learned this lesson the hard way. George and I had been learning a lot from a certain motivational speaker and we decided to fly to Florida to see him in person. He was the keynote speaker at a conference in the Orlando area.

We were mesmerized by his messages and his charismatic personality. After the meeting was over, he and his wife actually invited us into the "green room" to get to know us and share a meal together.

We felt so honoured that these people would associate with us - we felt like little wild flowers that got to bloom in their dazzling sunlight.

Just when we thought it couldn't get any better, they agreed to come to our city to be the keynote speakers for a conference we were hosting.

We were thrilled at the prospect of being friends with such influential people. Yet we were concerned that once they got to know us we wouldn't measure up to their standards. We felt the best way to secure a friendship with people so prestigious was to shower them with gifts and defer to them in every situation.

This strategy worked for a time but after a while, we were feeling depleted and resentful for always being the "givers" in the relationship. In reality, it wasn't their fault that we felt this way, it was our own insecurity and need for acceptance that caused our pain.

We were afraid to just be ourselves and tell them how we really felt for fear they would reject us. And in the end, once we made the decision to quit the ingratiating behaviour, that is exactly what happened. But amazingly, once we confronted our fear of rejection, we didn't feel any sense of loss - instead we had a profound sense of freedom.

Remember that your true friends are those who will celebrate your victories with you and cheer you on as you move towards developing your best self.

Though there will be people and situations that oppose us regaining our identity, the greatest enemies to fight are the self-limiting, self-sabotaging thoughts in our own minds. The real battle is not so much against the enemies without but against the enemies within.

There is a Japanese fish called koi that beautifully illustrates how thoughts determine your identity. Koi are domesticated, ornamental varieties of the carp fish that are kept for decorative purposes in outdoor ponds or water gardens. There are many varieties and they range in colour from white, black, red, yellow, blue, and cream. *14*

The amazing thing about koi is that they grow to the size of their surroundings. If they are in a small tank they will never grow longer than two or three inches. In a pond, they can grow up to ten inches long. In a large pond they can get up to eighteen inches long. But if they live in a huge lake where they can swim and stretch, they can grow up to three feet long. The size of the pond determines the size of the fish. 15

Just as the koi grow to the size of their pond, so we grow to the size of our thoughts. We must fight to expand our thoughts and our lives. One of the worst self-limiting thoughts we must resist if we are to grow into our fullest identity is complacency. Complacency is defined as: *a feeling of quiet pleasure or security, often while unaware of some potential danger or defect; self-satisfaction or smug satisfaction with an existing situation or condition. 16*

Popular American author and wilderness enthusiast Jon Krakauer is probably best known for his book *Into the Wild* which was adapted into a movie in 2007. Additionally, he also wrote *Into Thin Air* which reveals how Jon narrowly escaped death on a terrifying Mount Everest climb in 1996. He has this to say about complacency:

"So many people live within unhappy circumstances and yet will not take the initiative to change their situation because they are conditioned to a life of security, conformity, and conservatism, all of which may appear to give one peace of mind, but in reality nothing is more dangerous to the adventurous spirit within a man than a secure future. The very basic core of a man's living spirit is his passion for adventure. The joy of life comes from our encounters with new experiences, and hence there is no greater joy than to have an endlessly changing horizon, for each day to have a new and different sun." 17

> *"Nothing is more dangerous to the adventurous spirit within a man than a secure future."*

Whatever enemies stand between you and your true self, you must be as determined to vanquish them as Sir Winston Churchill was when he spoke these famous words in the House of Commons on May 13,1940 as Britain prepared to fight Adolf Hitler's regime of terror in WWII:

"We have before us an ordeal of the most grievous kind. We have before us many, many long months of struggle and of suffering. You ask, what is our policy? I can say: It is to wage war, by sea, land and air, with all our

might and with all the strength that God can give us; to wage war against a monstrous tyranny, never surpassed in the dark, lamentable catalogue of human crime. That is our policy. You ask, what is our aim? I can answer in one word: It is victory, victory at all costs, victory in spite of all terror, victory, however long and hard the road may be." 18

Just as in war we must fight to preserve our national freedom and identity, so in our own lives we must fight to preserve our personal freedom and identity. Many want the advantages and privileges of freedom but not all are prepared to fight the battles necessary to obtain it. Many desire to be free from the tyranny of a false identity but are unwilling to address the deep-rooted issues that hold them captive. Determine today to be one of the courageous few who are committed to keep fighting till complete victory is won.

9. CHAPTER NINE

TRIGGERS THAT CHALLENGE IDENTITY
WATCH WHAT HAPPENS WHEN I PUSH THIS...

Have you ever read *The Far Side* comics in the newspaper? They are generally a simple one-frame black and white sketch of a bizarre or satirical moment in either the animal or human world.

There is one *Far Side* comic in particular that perfectly illustrates the point of this chapter. In this comic you see an operating room with a group of surgeons and nurses around an anesthetized patient laying on the operating table. One of the surgeons is poking his finger into the patient's brain and the caption reads, "Whoa! That was a good one! Try it Hobbs - just poke his brain right where my finger is!" at which point you observe the patient's leg flying reflexively into the air. *1*

The patient has no control over the automatic reflex that occurs due to the stimulus of the slipshod surgeon's finger. Often we can feel helpless to control our reactions to negative stimuli in our lives. When certain people or situations "poke this", we often find ourselves in reaction mode to what are called psychological triggers.

This chapter is designed to equip you with practical tools to help you recognize and gain control over your response to these triggers. Without the ability to control your responses, you will never be free to make choices that move you towards your true identity. You will forever remain a victim to those things and people who "push your buttons". However, once you become aware of these triggers you will be better equipped to anticipate them and respond in a healthier way.

The University of Alberta Sexual Assault Centre explained a trigger as:

"... something that sets off a memory tape or flashback transporting the person back to the event of their original trauma."

Triggers are very personal; different things trigger different people. The survivor may begin to avoid situations and stimuli that they think trigger the flashback. They will react to this flashback trigger with an emotional intensity similar to that at the time of the trauma. A person's triggers are activated through one or more of the five senses: sight, sound, touch, smell and taste.

The senses identified as being the most common to trigger someone are sight and sound, followed by touch and smell, and taste close behind. A combination of the senses is identified as well, especially in situations that strongly resemble the original trauma. Although triggers are varied and diverse, there are often common themes. 2

Triggers can range in intensity depending on the trauma associated with it. A rape victim may be gripped with involuntary fear when she wants to share intimacy with a man. A child who suffered parental neglect may become obsessive in their adult relationships if they feel their partner pulling away. A successful businessman who grew up in extreme poverty may become intensely threatened by a sudden downturn in the markets.

No one is immune to triggers. We can be moving merrily along, enjoying our new sense of self for weeks, then suddenly, "Wham!", something happens that makes us blow up faster than a bag of microwave popcorn. Without warning you can find yourself drowning in a stormy sea of negative emotion, wondering what happened.

Sometimes triggers don't come directly from other people or external circumstances in your life. There are internal triggers that are more subtle and harder to identify. These triggers are usually ones that stem from our own self-perceptions developed during childhood.

For instance, while I was growing up my Mom was a great cook who excelled in baking. When I came through the front door after school, I was invariably met with the tantalizing aroma of any number of sweet delights - from fresh bread to cookies, cakes, and pies.

However, before we were allowed to indulge, we had to eat a healthy dinner. Dessert was the reward for finishing your vegetables. Desserts were also the reward of other desired behaviour - clean your room and we will go for ice cream; finish your chores and you can have some cookies; etcetera.

I subconsciously learned to associate food, particularly high carb food, with reward and comfort. To this day, when I am stressed I find myself looking through the junk food cupboard even though I'm not the slightest bit hungry. Stress can trigger me to seek comfort in food. I have learned to stop before I indulge in the M&M's and ask myself "What am I stressed about?"

Often the solution is as simple as picking up the phone and resolving some minor conflict; or it might be taking the time to do some unpleasant task I've been procrastinating. Whatever your subconscious trigger, the critical point is to recognize and address it rather than medicating it with food or any other form of avoidance.

Sometimes the triggers come from relationships. If you're honest you would have to admit that there are some people who just rub you the wrong way. They "push your buttons". Even when you tell yourself, "Today, I'm not going to let them upset me," before they even open their mouths, their mere presence grates on your nerves. And yet if someone asked you what it was about the person that irritated you so much, you couldn't even articulate it.

Janet had a very needy friend named Meghan. When they first met, Meghan seemed like a lot of fun. But after Meghan's boyfriend broke up with her, Janet felt like Meghan suddenly began sucking the life out of her - texting ten times a day, calling all the time, and leaving long mournful messages. Janet dreaded finally having to call her back because she knew she'd be trapped on the phone for hours while Meghan ranted on and on about her troubles.

Janet told herself she should be more compassionate. She berated herself for not being a better friend. But despite all her best efforts to adjust her attitude towards Meghan, she continually evoked all manner of undefined negative emotion within Janet.

After counselling with Janet we were able to identify a trigger that was activated by Meghan, which explained Janet's negative reaction to her neediness. Janet was very independent. She prided herself on not needing help from anybody. Meghan represented a disowned part of Janet's identity - vulnerability.

Because Janet had grown up in an environment that discouraged vulnerability and was emotionally sterile, she had learned that she needed to take care of herself. She despised feeling vulnerable and being needy in relationships. She sought to be assertive and in control in all her relationships.

She despised neediness in other people because it reflected a part of herself that she never wanted to surface. She believed that asking for help meant she was weak. Weakness made her vulnerable and she believed vulnerability set her up for pain.

But as we worked through the counselling process, Janet began to realize that pain also came from denying her true self any expression. In her case, pain came because she denied herself the opportunity to be vulnerable.

Though it was true she needed to establish boundaries with Meghan and others in her life who threatened to drain her emotionally, it was also true that there were other people in her life that she needed to "let in" - people who genuinely valued her individuality and wanted to help her when they sensed she was struggling. By refusing to acknowledge her needs and ask for help, she often felt isolated, overwhelmed, and exhausted.

Over time Janet began to accept that to need and to feel pain were an inescapable part of the human experience and part of her true identity. No amount of denial or self-preservation techniques could exempt her from it. Rather than trying to avoid pain she began to channel her energy towards understanding what triggered it and learned to develop a healthier response to it.

Identifying what triggers a reaction is the first step to managing your response. We can't control what happens to us, but we can control how we react to it. If we forfeit our power to choose a positive response, we will strengthen the trigger's ability to control us. As Eckhart Tolle said in his book *A New Earth: Awakening to Your Life's Purpose*:

"What you react to in another you strengthen within yourself. You can only be in a state of non-reaction if you can recognize someone's behaviour as coming from the ego, as being an expression of the collective human dysfunction. When you realize it's not personal, there is no longer a compulsion to react as if it were." 3

"What you react to in another you strengthen within yourself.

Triggers can elicit an automatic response that we may feel powerless to control. Yet even in the most dire of circumstances we are never without the ability to choose how we react, as evidenced in the following story recorded in a courtroom in South Africa:

A frail black woman about seventy years old slowly rises to her feet. Across the room and facing her are several white police officers. One of them is Mr. Van der Broek, who has just been tried and found implicated in the murders of both the woman's son and her husband some years before. Van der Broek had come to the woman's home, taken her son, shot him at point blank range and then set the young man's body on fire while he and his officers partied nearby.

Several years later, Van der Broek and his men had returned for her husband as well. For months she knew nothing of his whereabouts. Then almost two years after her husband's disappearance, Van der Broek came back to fetch the woman herself. How well she remembers in vivid detail that evening, going to a place beside a river where she was shown her husband, bound and beaten, but still strong in spirit, lying on a pile of wood. The last words she heard from his lips as the officers poured gasoline over his body and set him aflame were, "Father, forgive them… "

Now the woman stands in the courtroom and listens to the confessions offered by Mr. Van der Broek. A member of South Africa's Truth and Reconciliation Commission turns to her and asks, "So what do you want? How should justice be done to this man who has so brutally destroyed your family?"

"I want three things," begins the old woman calmly, but confidently. "I want first to be taken to the place where my husband's body was burned so that I can gather up the dust and give his remains a decent burial."

She paused, then continued. "My husband and son were my only family, I want secondly, therefore, for Mr. Van der Broek to become my son. I would like for him to come twice a month to the ghetto and spend a day with me so that I can pour out on him whatever love I still have remaining in me."

She also stated that she wanted a third thing, "This is also the wish of my husband. And so, I would kindly ask someone to come to my side and lead me across the courtroom so that I can take Mr. Van der Broek in my arms and embrace him and let him know that he is truly forgiven." As the court assistant came to lead the elderly woman across the room, Mr. Van der Broek, overwhelmed by what he had just heard, fainted. As he did, those in the courtroom, family, friends, neighbours - all victims of decades of oppression and injustice - began to sing softly but assuredly, "Amazing grace, how sweet the sound, that saved a wretch like me." 4

This precious woman had learned through suffering indescribable pain that she still had the power to choose her response. She would have been completely justified in responding in anger and bitterness and demanding vengeance for all that she had endured. Instead, she chose to respond in mercy and forgiveness. Her response demonstrated not weakness but strength. She understood that bitterness was a poison that, if she drank, would kill her, not her oppressor.

She refused to be a prisoner to her pain, releasing not only Van der Broek but herself from a lifetime of bondage. She refused to be defined as another victim of racism - that was not her identity. Her identity was not in what had happened to her but in what she chose to be.

Bryant McGill, in his book *Simple Reminders: Inspiration for Living Your Best Life* affirms this woman's wise choice:

> *"When you blame others, you are affirming that you have no power, and your existence is only a reaction to the power of others."* 5

Rather than getting discouraged by the fact that people are predictable in their selfish nature, why not use that knowledge to your advantage? Recognize that people aren't purposely doing something to you - they are simply living out of their own need for self-preservation.

When you consider how much of a challenge it is to change yourself, you will begin to grasp what an utterly futile exercise it is to try to change someone else. This knowledge should free you to simply accept people where they're at and not take everything as a personal attack. Once you extricate yourself from a defensive, reactive position you can take positive action and move towards your best self.

> *When you consider how much of a challenge it is to change yourself, you will begin to grasp what an utterly futile exercise it is to try to change someone else.*

Knowing we are powerless to change the people and situations around us does not make us victims. It empowers us to confidently channel our energy where it will be productive - in shaping our own appropriate responses and developing a strong personal identity.

American bestselling author, speaker, and behavioural science academic Dr. Steve Maraboli had this to say about rising above the things that would stop you from becoming the person you were meant to be:

"Today is a new day. Don't let your history interfere with your destiny! Let today be the day you stop being a victim of your circumstances and start taking action towards the life you want. You have the power and the time to shape your life. Break free from the poisonous victim mentality and embrace the truth of your greatness. You were not meant for a mundane or mediocre life!" 6

10. CHAPTER TEN

STOP THE BLEEDING DEVELOP AND PRACTICE SELF-CARE

"Boom!" Another ominous crack of thunder resounds as you drive nervously through blinding sheets of rain. In vain your wiper blades flail wildly, trying to clear your windshield long enough for you to inch your way home through the stormy night. Suddenly, amidst the downpour, your eyes meet with a nauseating sight - the wreckage of two vehicles - an SUV and a semi-trailer hauling cattle are strewn across the highway. You pull your car to the shoulder, call 911, and scramble towards the grisly scene.

Coached by the 911 operator you set about the gruesome task of establishing triage - which injuries need immediate medical attention and which will have to wait. Amidst the mournful bellowing of maimed and bleeding livestock you make your way to the semi cab. Thankfully you discover the driver is unharmed and you quickly turn your attention towards the crumpled SUV and its occupant.

A young male victim is screaming in agony, pinned by the steering wheel. His femur is protruding through his thigh, but thankfully the femoral artery is not severed. As you administer first aid, you suddenly notice the man is somewhat confused and his speech is becoming incoherent. Within a few minutes he loses consciousness. Instantly your focus changes from the initial superficial wounds, as you recognize the first priority is now a life-threatening head injury.

When the paramedics arrive you tell them all you know and ask if the young man is going to make it. They assure you that he will live, but with the injuries he sustained, his mental and physical capabilities will be severely affected and he will have to undergo extensive rehabilitation.

Often the most debilitating injuries to our identity are not immediately identified as they can be easily overshadowed by the superficial bleeding of our emotions. For instance, a poor quarterly review from your employer can evoke profuse emotional "bleeding" in regards to job security. However the more critical and not so easily identified wound has actually been dealt to your identity.

If your identity is tied to your job, then you will feel lost without it. It's important to know "you" are not a social worker, plumber, or an engineer. You are a person who does social work, plumbing, or engineering. You will still be you - regardless of your profession. The unique giftedness that brought you to where you are will be what takes you to the next place you need to be.

Once we "stop the bleeding" in our emotions, there are often deeper identity issues that require long term rehabilitation in order to achieve a full recovery. Part of the long term identity rehabilitation process is developing a healthy system of self-care.

Only after you are in a healthy emotional state are you actually capable of helping others achieve the same.

What is self-care? The University at Buffalo School of Social Work defines it this way:

"Self-care is an essential ... survival skill. Self-care refers to activities and practices that we can engage in on a regular basis to reduce stress and maintain and enhance our short- and longer-term health and well-being." 1

Self-care is just as the term indicates: you are caring for yourself. You are taking responsibility for your own mental, emotional, physical, and spiritual well-being. You don't consider it to be a selfish act but something beneficial you do, not only for yourself but for others. When you are whole and strong in your identity, other people are not forced to walk on eggshells around you, nor are they compelled to constantly affirm you in an effort to make you feel better about yourself. Only after you are in a healthy emotional state are you actually capable of helping others achieve the same.

The Dean of Social Work at the University of Buffalo, Nancy J. Smyth, PhD., expressed the concept of self-care so succinctly:

"Just like you do on a plane, you need to put on your own oxygen mask first before trying to help others." 2

Just as every person is unique, so must every self-care plan be uniquely suited for the individual. What works for me may not work for you. However, there are some general principles that should be incorporated into every effective self-care plan to help you move towards a healthy identity.

The list below is simply a guide to help stimulate you to create a self-care plan that works for you. Take the time to examine your own life to decide what you need. Start with one or two goals and allow yourself time to truly incorporate them into your everyday life. If you try to make too many changes all at once, you will likely get overwhelmed and give up on the whole process.

SPIRITUAL SELF-CARE

Earlier we explained how the spiritual part of our identity is like the engine of a car. It needs regular maintenance to stay in tip-top shape. There are many ways to rejuvenate your spirit - a peaceful walk through nature, reading an inspirational book, attending church, spending time in quiet prayer and meditation, or even listening to uplifting music. The importance of spiritual self-care cannot be stressed enough. Spiritual self-care is the foundation on which you will build any other area of self-care.

PHYSICAL SELF-CARE

FOOD

A regular diet of healthy nutritious food is a basic requirement if we are to feel our best. In a fast-paced life it is tempting to substitute real food with highly processed fast food. One self-care goal in this area could be to plan a menu for one week of healthy meals and snacks. Go to the grocery store and buy all the necessary ingredients. Purging your cupboards of the unhealthy fast food will also help you not to succumb to old less healthy eating patterns. 3

EXERCISE

A recent study conducted by the Canadian Society for Exercise Physiology recommends that adults aged eighteen to sixty-four years should accumulate at least one hundred fifty minutes of moderate to vigorous intensity aerobic physical activity per week, in bouts of ten minutes or more. This would translate into thirty minutes a day, five days a week. It is also recommended to add muscle and bone strengthening activities using major muscle groups at least two days per week.

Following these guidelines can reduce the risk of premature death, coronary heart disease, stroke, hypertension, colon cancer, breast cancer, type two diabetes, and osteoporosis as well as improve fitness and body composition and even improve mental health. *4*

We all know we should be physically active, but we usually have more excuses than execution. Remember that the key in self-care is always to start small. If you can't see how you can do thirty minutes a day, start with a quick fifteen minute walk at lunchtime twice a week. Do this consistently for three weeks and you will have formed a new healthy self-care habit that you can build on.

SLEEP

Although everyone has different needs, a reasonable guideline is that most people need between seven and ten hours of sleep per night. One example of a self-care goal could be: I will go to bed by ten-thirty p.m. during the week so that I can get enough sleep.

MEDICAL

Prevention is always better than cure. Beyond ensuring regular visits to your doctor, dentist, and optometrist, treating yourself to a monthly massage may be a self-care goal that you would benefit from.

EMOTIONAL SELF-CARE

COUNSELLING

If we are developing a stronger sense of identity, we will be better equipped to resolve most of life's problems that arise. However there may be times where we find ourselves feeling overwhelmed. Self-care at this juncture could mean seeing a psychologist, a clinical social worker, a minister, or a therapist. It could also mean talking to a trusted friend or family member. Often we process our thoughts better as we verbalize them. A compassionate listening ear is sometimes all we need to find our way through our problems. A self-care goal could be to seek out an individual you trust who is willing to be that listening ear and schedule a time to meet with them.

KEEPING A JOURNAL

Keeping a journal of your emotions and thoughts along the way can also be a powerful tool for self-discovery. Something wonderful happens when you get your thoughts and feelings out of your head and onto paper - you can stop them from circling incessantly inside your mind and hold them still long enough to examine them. Invariably, once you see them on paper, you can identify illogical reasoning and come up with simple solutions to issues that may have been nagging you for months. A self-care goal could be writing in your journal at least three times per week.

I have personally benefitted greatly from the journalling process. It has helped me to silence the inner critic in my subconscious mind. Negative thoughts about myself were constantly floating through my mind like the background music in a department store. Journalling turned up the volume on this background noise and made it possible for me to rationally assess, challenge, and replace the negative thoughts with positive ones.

SELF-TALK

We've already discussed this at length in Chapter Six, so we won't go into great detail here except to say that self-talk is an important part of self-care. Self-talk can be audible, but most of the time it is simply an internal conversation we have with ourselves. Journalling, as we mentioned above, will help to make us aware of our negative thoughts towards ourselves and correct them. A self-care goal in this area may be to practice saying one complimentary thing out loud to yourself each day.

LEISURE TIME

The bane of our modern existence is over-busyness. Margaret Fuller wisely stated:

> *"Men for the sake of getting a living forget to live."* 5

We need to schedule our recreation time just like we do our professional appointments. In the same way a field will produce more bountifully after a season of rest, so you will be more productive if you make time to do things you enjoy. A goal in this area might be to schedule a date night with your partner once a week, join a sport club, or enroll in an art class - whatever fuels your passion.

LAUGHTER

According to the Cancer Treatment Centers of America, laughter can provide all kinds of benefits such as boost the immune and circulatory systems; relax muscles throughout the body; trigger the release of endorphins (the body's natural painkillers); balance blood pressure; improve mental functions (alertness, memory, creativity); reduce stress; and improve sleep. The great news is that you don't have to wait till something strikes your funny bone to enjoy the benefits of laughter. Your body will respond to "practiced" laughter as well as it does to spontaneous laughter. A self-care goal may be to join a Laughter Therapy group, watch more comic shows and movies, spend more time with children; or just practice laughing in front of a mirror. *6*

RELATIONSHIPS

The people in our lives greatly influence our identity and how we feel about ourselves. It has been said that people will either add, subtract, multiply, or divide you. It is critical to discern which people in your life contribute to your well-being and which people diminish it. Limit your contact with those who deplete you. It may not mean cutting them out of your life entirely, especially if it's a family member, but you will need to establish firm boundaries with these people. Remember the old saying holds true: "You can never soar with the eagles if you are always hanging out with turkeys."

> *"You can never soar with the eagles if you are always hanging out with turkeys."*

Screen your phone calls and don't be afraid to say, "No". Avoid being alone with those who drain you, but if you must, let them know prior to your meeting when you have to leave. Remind yourself that practicing self-care is not being selfish - it's a survival skill. Eleanor Brown wisely stated:

> *"Self-care isn't selfish (it is a gift to all concerned). You can't serve from an empty vessel."* 7

A self-care goal in relationships may be to schedule a weekly coffee date with a friend who genuinely cares about you and wants to support you in becoming your best self.

If you want to have a strong sense of identity, you will need to make self-care a priority, not something that happens (or doesn't happen) by accident. However, as we said at the beginning of this chapter, start slow. Begin with one or two areas that you know need the most work. Once you do, you will feel empowered to take even bolder steps toward the person you desire to be. *8*

Victoria Moran is someone who learned through personal experience the benefits of self-care. She struggled for years with obesity till she began to pursue becoming the person she desired to be. Her life was transformed and she has since become a bestselling author, an inspirational speaker, and a certified holistic health counsellor appearing twice on *The Oprah Winfrey Show*. She had this to say about the dedication to self-care that is required to become your best self: *9*

"Growing into your future with health and grace and beauty doesn't have to take all your time. It rather requires a dedication to caring for yourself as if you were rare and precious, which you are, and regarding all life around you as equally so, which it is." 10

Daniell Koepke is another great example of someone who had to learn healthy self-care in order to discover and realize her full potential. From the time she was a teenager she battled anorexia and bulimia and all the mental anguish that accompanies these eating disorders. In 2009, while Daniell was in treatment, she decided to start a blog called the Internal Acceptance Movement (I.A.M.) which began as an effort to raise awareness for eating disorders. Now I.A.M. has grown into a movement that Daniell hopes will "help people heal, from any mental health struggle or insecurity, to remind others that they aren't alone in their battle, and to remind them that things can and will get better." *11*

This courageous young woman spoke these inspiring words about her struggle for identity:

"Most of my life has been spent trying to shrink myself. Trying to become smaller. Quieter. Less sensitive. Less opinionated. Less needy. Less me. Because I didn't want to be a burden. I didn't want to be too much or push people away. I wanted people to like me. I wanted to be cared for and valued. I wanted to be wanted. So for years, I sacrificed myself for the sake of making other people happy. And for years, I suffered. But I'm tired of suffering, and I'm done shrinking. It's not my job to change who I am in order to become someone else's idea of a worthwhile human being. I am worthwhile. Not because other people think I am, but because I exist, and therefore I matter. My thoughts matter. My feelings matter. My voice matters. And with or without anyone's permission or approval, I will continue to be who I am and speak my truth. Even if it makes people angry. Even if it makes them uncomfortable. Even if they choose to leave. I refuse to shrink. I choose to take up space. I choose to honour my feelings. I choose to give myself permission to get my needs met. I choose to make self-care a priority. I choose me." 12

If we are ever going to become our authentic self - that person we dream of being - we will have to be tenacious and unapologetic about nurturing ourselves. Like a swiftly flowing mountain stream, your life is flowing by with each moment that passes. I urge you to be bold enough to diligently protect and to freely drink from those refreshing waters before they cease to flow.

11. CHAPTER ELEVEN

RECONNECTING TO YOUR TRUE IDENTITY

> *"Can you remember who you were before the world told you who you should be?" 1*
>
> *Unknown*

Donna began her day like many others. She got out of bed at about five-thirty a.m. and went to let out her dog, Nikki. Walking toward the door, she felt really odd. She then made some coffee and went to call Nikki back in. But the words that came out weren't what she was trying to say.

"That was weird," she thought. "Did I hear that right?"

Chalking it up to the early hour, she went on with her morning routine. Yet the odd feeling went on, as well. She couldn't quite explain it. Things were just fuzzy. She knew something was wrong medically and even wondered, “Is this what a stroke feels like?” It was a strange situation for her as a clinical nurse. She knew the warning signs, she had seen evolving stroke symptoms in patients, but facing them herself, there was an eerie disbelief - especially considering she was only twenty-seven and in overall good health.

With all of those thoughts going through her head, she drove to her office. As she started her workday, the fuzzy feeling continued. Eventually, she turned to her boss and said, “I think I am having a stroke.”

He thought she was kidding. As the morning went on, he realized she wasn’t. Her symptoms piled up: Drooling; weakness in her left arm, then in her left leg; finally, her speech slurred so much that it was unintelligible. By the time she reached the emergency room, she could no longer speak.

Donna knew exactly, precisely, and in great detail everything that was going on around her.

Everything she’d studied and heard from stroke patients was playing out. She felt no pain - only anguish. She was painfully alert, trapped inside a body that would not work and could not communicate. She formed thoughts and sentences but could do nothing with them.

Her mind raced. She wondered what her life would be like in this new, isolated state. She wondered, “How would I care for patients? Could I even do the work that brought me such joy?”

She felt an intense loneliness - like no one could understand what was happening to her, and that no one ever would be able to really understand her again.

Three days before, she had undergone a small, routine procedure. It went fine, but what she didn’t know was that she had a condition that left her prone to clotting after surgery. Sure enough, clots had formed around the mitral valve in her heart. Over the course of that fateful morning, some of those clots broke off and traveled to the temporal lobe of her brain, creating many small lesions. She saw them on the MRI – white speckles that lit up her brain like brilliant stars lighting up the sky.

However, Donna was fortunate in so many ways. She suffered no long-term paralysis. Her speech returned, and eventually she relearned the things that were stored in the parts of her brain which she had lost.

Losing a part of your brain is not like losing your memory. You retain the knowledge that you know how to do simple tasks - such as read a calendar, walk on a treadmill, or weigh a patient on a balance beam scale - but the processes for doing those things have been wiped clean from your brain.

It was startling to discover these black holes. Relearning these things took time and patience, but with the love and kindness of others as well as sheer determination Donna got her life back. She relearned all the little things and continued with the big things she had planned for herself both personally and professionally.

After her ordeal, Donna shared these inspiring words: *"I'm here to tell everyone who is recovering from a stroke or helping a loved one recover that there is hope. You may be dealing with those same feelings of isolation, doubt, and despair I was feeling. You may be fighting through the pain and fear of rehabilitation, or coming to grips with the understanding that some of your abilities may be different now. But don't give up. You can get your life back after a stroke. Not only that, you can go on to accomplish a great deal."* 2

Donna K. Arnett, Ph.D., is now a noted researcher and chairperson of the Department of Epidemiology at the University of Alabama at Birmingham School of Public Health. Her life is a living testimony to the fact that no matter how devastating the effects of a stroke, it is possible to recover and live a full life.

The disconnection, isolation, and subsequent despair experienced by stroke victims is much like the experience of an individual who recognizes they've lost touch with their true identity. You may identify with the feelings of disconnection and isolation. You may feel trapped inside a person who has lost the ability to communicate your true feelings or to do the things you really want to do. You may feel despair because nobody around you understands you.

But there is hope. The person you truly desire to be is not lost - he or she is still buried deep inside you. Like a precious diamond hidden beneath a mountain of rock, it will take a lot of time, effort, and determination to recover yourself. But don't be afraid of the pain and the struggle. The reward of unearthing the diamond will be worth it. As you begin to witness its multifaceted brilliance, you will be able to embrace, and even rejoice, in the toil of the mining process.

Elisabeth Kubler-Ross said:

"The most beautiful people we have known are those who have known defeat, known suffering, known struggle, known loss, and have found their way out of the depths. These persons have an appreciation, a sensitivity and an understanding of life that fills them with compassion, gentleness, and a deep loving concern. Beautiful people do not just happen." 3

You may sincerely desire to be one of those beautiful people that Ms. Kubler-Ross described, but do not know where to start. Stroke victims visit therapists who help them in their rehabilitation process. But for those seeking to regain a lost identity, it may not be so easy to know where to get help. While this is not an exhaustive list, these are a few practical things to help you re-establish that connection and find your way back to your true self:

WAYS TO RE-CONNECT TO YOUR TRUE SELF:

1. FILL YOUR MIND WITH INFORMATION THAT WILL BUILD YOUR IDENTITY AND SELF-ESTEEM.

It has been said that where the mind goes, so goes the person. Without question, the quality of your life is determined by your most dominant thoughts. If you are serious about reconnecting to your best self, then you must be discriminating about what you allow your mind to focus on. Focusing on what you have lost is counterproductive. Instead, focus on what you desire to become. Reading inspiring

> *The quality of your life is determined by your most dominant thoughts.*

books, attending positive seminars, viewing uplifting media sites, talking to confident people, and watching movies that inspire you are all avenues that can awaken your identity. *4*

Your current thoughts have brought you to where you are now and how you view yourself. You must take the responsibility to create new thoughts if you want to see yourself differently.

"Who looks outside, dreams; who looks inside, awakes." 5

Carl Gustav Jung

2. DEVELOP SELF-UNDERSTANDING AND A REALISTIC SELF-EVALUATION.

To establish a strong sense of identity, you need to develop a realistic versus an emotional evaluation of yourself. Try to see yourself through the eyes of someone who is non-judgmental such as a therapist as you seek to discover your true identity. Have a "therapy session" with yourself. Pour out your beliefs about yourself through self-talk and/or journalling and examine them objectively as a counsellor would. Understand the past and how it has influenced you, but don't be limited or victimized by it - rise above it. Make an unbiased list of your strengths and weaknesses and choose to focus on your strengths.

People often make the mistake of focusing on their weaknesses in an effort to improve and "balance" them against their strengths. But imagine if you were right-handed and you broke your right arm. During the six-week healing process, you would be forced to use your left hand. Initially, your handwriting would be barely legible, but after a few weeks it would improve significantly. However, as soon as the cast came off you would undoubtedly revert back to your right hand: it is stronger, therefore it would be absurd not to use it.

Don't waste your life trying to "fix" yourself. Recognize and celebrate who you really are. Develop your strengths so you can realize your identity's fullest potential. Your true self doesn't exist in your weaknesses but in your strengths.

> *"You have been criticizing yourself for years, and it hasn't worked. Try approving of yourself and see what happens."* 6
>
> *Louise L. Hay*

3. PURSUE REALISTIC GOALS.

One of the most demoralizing things that can erode a person's confidence in themselves is trying to achieve unrealistic goals. That's why it's critical you take the time to develop self-understanding as in the previous point. It will enable you to readily identify realistic goals that draw on your strengths and unrealistic goals which drag you into your weaknesses. It is also helpful to discuss your goals with a trusted counsellor or friend - someone who will tell you the truth, even if it's not what you want to hear.

There is a popular psychological theory which proposes, "You can be anything you decide to be." Initially it sounds like a very positive, empowering concept and one that would contribute to a strong sense of self. However, in many cases it actually has the opposite effect.

While it is true that you could be anything you choose to be, you may not enjoy being that person. Career satisfaction research reveals that over seventy percent of people are unhappy in their current job. For instance you may become a lawyer because you want to enjoy the lifestyle that a lawyer's salary affords. However, if this career choice does not utilize your strengths, then you will never excel in your profession and you will join the ranks of the seventy percent who dread going to work each day.

Rather than deciding your goals by outward factors such as a desire for money, acceptance, or pursuits beyond your natural ability, choose goals in line with your true self - that is where your strength, passion, and abilities will come to life.

Once you have chosen a realistic, self-affirming goal, you will need to break it down into shorter attainable ones. For example, if your long-range goal is to leave your current job and pursue a career you believe is more in line with who you are, then you will need a series of practical short-term goals along the way. You may need to start by paying off any credit card debts you have so that you can afford to make a career change. Start with the card with the smallest outstanding balance. Once it's paid off, move to the card with the next smallest balance, and so on till you've reached your goal.

On this journey, be your own best encourager. Reward yourself for every accomplishment, no matter how small. With every short-term goal achieved, you will gain confidence to keep moving towards becoming the person you believe yourself to be.

> *"The mystery of human existence lies not in just staying alive, but in finding something to live for."* 7
>
> *Fyodor Dostoyevsky, The Brothers Karamazov*

4. GUARD AGAINST NEGATIVITY.

It is tragically ironic that we spend so much of our lives wishing they were better and wishing we were happier, yet all the while we are entertaining negative thoughts and speaking pessimistic, critical words. Doing so is equivalent to complaining about how polluted the drinking water is while we continue to dump toxic chemicals into it. Negativity pollutes our lives and the search for our identity.

Author Taite Adams has this to say about negativity:

> *"Negative thinking will not produce positive changes - ever."* 8

If you want to break free from the false persona you've been trapped in and begin to live out your true identity, then you will need to guard against negativity. It's not easy to stay positive. Life is not always fair and people are not always kind. We don't always make the right choices, and it's easy to live in the land of regret. But when things go bad, don't go bad with them. Forgiveness is a gift you give yourself. Learn to resist critical, bitter, or resentful thoughts and cultivate positive regard towards yourself and others.

One simple exercise that will help build a positive mindset is to practice giving sincere compliments. This causes you to actively focus on the good qualities in people and in the world around you. And when someone offers you a compliment, learn to accept it graciously. Deflecting positive reinforcement is counterproductive to a healthy identity.

Another way to counteract negativity is to reshape adverse memories that have damaged your identity. Being fired is ranked at the top of the list of experiences that can negatively affect your self-image. However, you can reshape these negative memories by choosing to focus on the good that could come as a result of being fired. When this memory is triggered, instead of rehearsing and talking about how unjustly you were treated, remind yourself of how you no longer have to live under the stress of the situation; talk about how you are free to pursue a better career and the new relationships you will be able to build which could become the key to unlocking your fullest potential. By reshaping your memory, you are reshaping your future.

"The reason negative emotions burn out so very slowly in us is because we keep igniting them with old, unpleasant memories." 9

Ali B. Moe

5. SEEK OUT GROUP SUPPORT AND SOCIAL INTERACTION.

Though we live in a time when human interaction is being replaced with technology, human beings remain intrinsically social creatures. We don't thrive in isolation. Just as flowers need cross-pollination to blossom, so we become more beautiful and fruitful with the cross-pollination of other healthy individuals.

Make it a priority to build relationships with people and social groups that share your passion for self-development. Seek an environment where you are accepted and feel a sense of belonging. Once you find it, take the risk of opening yourself up and building trust with the people you meet there.

Toni Collette is an Australian actress best known for her role in the movie *About a Boy* (2002). She very insightfully commented on how we crave yet are afraid to develop meaningful relationships. She said that if we actually have the courage to do so, we will connect with our true selves:

"People are so fearful about opening themselves up. All you want to do is to be able to connect with other people. When you connect with other people, you connect with something in yourself. It makes you feel happy. And yet it's so scary - it makes people feel vulnerable and unsafe." 10

When you connect with other people, you connect with something in yourself.

Defy your fear. Dare to connect and discover that part of yourself that can only be seen in the face of a trusted friend.

6. EXPERIMENT.

"The purpose of life is to live it, to taste experience to the utmost, to reach out eagerly and without fear for newer and richer experience." 11

Eleanor Roosevelt

It may seem redundant to say that if you're not satisfied with who you are at present, it's time to try something new. However, in my many years of experience in counselling people, even the most obvious reason for our dissatisfaction is often overlooked. But as the old adage says: "If the horse is dead, for goodness sake dismount!"

If you are growing in your identity, things that used to bring you great enjoyment will now be unsatisfying to you. Things that once ignited your passion will be dull and tedious. You will need to experiment in order to find new things that stimulate you to keep you moving towards your fullest potential.

Try a new hobby, visit places you've never been, meet new people, seek out new ideas. New experiences will help determine where your passion lies and unlock clues to your expanding identity.

This is not the time to be picky - this is the time to throw caution to the wind and try something totally outside your box. You may be surprised to discover what you may enjoy if you give it a chance.

Years ago I thought that football was one of the most unintelligible sports to watch on television. Then I moved to a football-frenzied city, became friends with some of the players and coaches, and actually went to the games. To my great surprise I loved it! Now I can hardly wait for football season and, more importantly, I have gained lifelong friends that have positively shaped my identity through the process.

"Try a thing you haven't done three times. Once, to get over the fear of doing it. Twice, to learn how to do it. And a third time to figure out whether you like it or not." 12

Virgil Thomson

7. BE WILLING TO RISK FAILURE.

Everyone who has heard the name Michael Jordan knows of the iconic success he had in his career. His biography on the NBA website states: "By acclamation, Michael Jordan is the greatest basketball player of all time." *13*

But what many people don't know is that his tremendous success came only after a devastating failure. Jordan was cut from his high school basketball team. Despite the painful failure and what his coaches told him, young Michael was willing to take a risk to pursue who he believed himself to be - a basketball player. Michael is quoted as saying:

> *"I can accept failure, everyone fails at something. But I can't accept not trying." 14*

If we are ever to discover and live out of our true identity, we will have to be willing to risk failure. We may not succeed on the first attempt. The fear of failure is often what keeps people trapped in an existence far below their dreams and their potential. A poll taken of people over the age of seventy revealed that the number one thing that they regretted was that they never took the risks and did what was necessary to become the people they truly desired to be.

How do you overcome fear and become willing to take a risk? "Just do it!" as Nike says. Joyce Meyer says: "Do it afraid!" If you wait till fear subsides, then you may wait your whole life. Yes, calculate the risk and analyze the data, but at some point you must take action. Fear will not leave by willpower alone, but it will run from a person of action.

> *Fear will not leave by willpower alone, but it will run from a person of action.*

Remember that failure is not final but regret is.

8. PAY IT FORWARD.

Paying it forward is an ideology made popular by the 2000 movie *Pay it Forward* starring Helen Hunt, Kevin Spacey, and child star Haley Joel Osment. Usually the concept of paying it forward is viewed in light of doing good deeds for others so

> *There are treasures within you that will never be unlocked till you connect with people who need what you have inside you. These people are the key that will unlock your true identity.*

that those kind acts will return to us when we are in need. But it is a principle that also applies to re-connecting with your best self.

Winston Churchill said:

"We make a living by what we get. We make a life by what we give." 15

While you can learn much about who you are by looking within yourself, there are some parts of your identity that can only be found by looking outside yourself and investing in other people. There are treasures within you that will never be unlocked till you connect with people who need what you have inside you. These people are the key that will unlock your true identity.

Louis Pasteur's best self came to light when he developed vaccinations in an effort to help those who suffered from diseases such as rabies and anthrax. Johannes Gutenberg was a simple goldsmith till his best self found a way to make books available for all people. His subsequent invention of the printing press changed the modern world and afforded him the honour of being regarded as "one of the most influential people in human history". *16*

Mother Theresa was a simple nun till she saw the great needs of the destitute on the streets of Calcutta. Her true identity blossomed as she inspired over forty-five hundred sisters in one hundred thirty-three countries to run all kinds of benevolent works such as hospices and homes for people with HIV/AIDS, leprosy, and tuberculosis. They also oversaw soup kitchens, medical dispensaries, and mobile clinics; sponsored children and family counselling programs, and built orphanages and schools for the poor - all because one little woman found her identity in helping others. *17*

> *You will discover your greatest abilities and passions when you seek to unlock someone else's.*

You will discover your greatest abilities and passions when you seek to unlock someone else's. A mother's fervent love and desire for her child to live to their fullest potential will bring the best out of herself. A teacher who desires to empower his students with knowledge and wisdom will be equally inspired to excel in these same qualities himself.

"As we work to create light for others, we naturally light our own way." 18

Mary Anne Radmacher

Look for opportunities to pay it forward. It can be as simple as speaking a kind word to someone who is discouraged; extending forgiveness to someone; mowing your neighbour's lawn; or visiting a lonely senior citizen. As you pay it forward, you can be assured that the light you create for others will brighten the path to rediscovering your best self.

9. ACCEPT THE MULTIPLICITY OF YOUR IDENTITY.

One of the biggest hindrances to re-connecting to our identities is the resistance we have to accepting unpleasantness about ourselves. Somewhere we have believed the lie that if we are to *be* good we must always *appear* and *behave* good. However, if we are ever to embrace our true identity we must first accept the multiplicity of our identity. We are never completely wonderful, nor are we ever completely abominable - we are curiously and uniquely a mixture of both.

The best way to describe the multiplicity of our identity is to look at a tree. It is always a tree, but it changes with the seasons and it doesn't always look or behave the same. The tree has no control over the seasons, but it has learned to adapt to them. The tree is not embarrassed by its unsightly appearance due to its loss of leaves in the fall. It knows this is an essential part of surviving the winter. It is powerless to pull up its roots and run south to escape the bitter cold. But it also knows that eventually the snow will melt and winter will give way to the warmth of spring. Summer will then bring out its full luxurious appearance and it will bear fruit once again.

So it is with ourselves. We have no control over the seasons of our lives, therefore we must learn to embrace our adaptations to the seasons. When winter hits our lives, we may not look lush and green, but we must learn to appreciate ourselves even in our nakedness. We can't run away from nor exorcise the parts of ourselves we don't like. We sometimes feel barren and leafless; we sometimes feel green and fruitful. But we should be OK with ourselves in whatever season we find ourselves. Learn to esteem and accept yourself completely - the good, the bad, and the ugly - that's who you really are.

Stacey Charter has achieved notoriety by creating numerous quotations on life, happiness, and inspiration after enduring both divorce and cancer. Many of Charter's quotes have been printed and distributed online.[19]

She once wisely said:

"Don't rely on someone else for your happiness and self-worth. Only you can be responsible for that. If you can't love and respect yourself – no one else will be able to make that happen. Accept who you are – completely; the good and the bad – and make changes as YOU see fit – not because you think someone else wants you to be different." [20]

"Don't rely on someone else for your happiness and self-worth. Only you can be responsible for that.

Remember that reconnecting to your identity is a journey, not a destination. Enjoy the journey. You may not be where you want to be, or even where you think you ought to be, but be thankful you are not where you used to be. You're OK and you're on your way.

10. DREAM AGAIN.

Today I enjoyed a beautiful mid-summer's afternoon. As per my usual routine, I set about to write another chapter in the book you are reading. However, I was seduced by the warmth of the sunshine and the music of the song birds in the backyard. Uncharacteristically I chose to delay my writing to indulge in the sights and sounds of nature, if only for a few minutes. As I stretched out on the lawn and my eyes travelled up to the sky, I was captured by the sight of something that magically transported me back to my childhood - cottony white clouds drifting lazily across a brilliant blue sky.

How many childhood afternoons have you spent in this mesmerizing activity as dazzling white dragons swallowed ambling, fluffy centaurs only to have them both melt into an enormous mythical unicorn? These were days when our imaginations carried us to untold adventures and enchanted places where we were the heroes of our dreams.

In this brief reverie, I was reminded of the importance of taking time to dream in recovering our lost identity. As adults our lives are so enslaved by the necessities of life that we have essentially lost the art of dreaming, and with it the ability to connect with our true selves.

Gloria Steinem described the indispensable nature of dreaming by stating:

"Without leaps of imagination or dreaming, we lose the excitement of possibilities. Dreaming, after all is a form of planning." 21

If your analytical self has logically and systematically put a stranglehold on pursuing the dreams that once inspired you, then it's time for your imaginative self to take back some control in your life and allow your dreams to open new opportunities for you.

You may be reading this and thinking, "I've tried to follow my dreams in the past and they turned into nightmares! I am not interested in putting myself out there only to get hurt again."

Don't allow your past to steal your future. Don't trade your dreams for mediocrity.

In the pursuit of your dreams, it's critical that you understand the difference between a dream and a fantasy. A dream is something that requires determination to bring it to reality. A fantasy takes no effort at all because it is simply a delusion - there is no reality or substance to it. A dream demands your focus. A fantasy distracts your focus. A dream will motivate you to action. A fantasy anesthetizes you - you lose awareness of reality and your ability to function. A dream will challenge all your fears, test all your limits, and cause you to rise to your fullest potential. This is not an easy task. The road to success is lined with many tempting parking places.

But as *New York Times* bestselling author and leadership speaker Orrin Woodward said:

> *"You won't find your dream until you lose your excuses. Licking your wounds will not stop the bleeding, but applying pressure will."* 22

Living your dreams and discovering your true identity are worth the fight. Just consider the alternative - never realizing your greatest abilities, forfeiting life-changing relationships and opportunities, renouncing everything you ever truly desired, existing but never really living.

In spite of what you have gone through or are going through, dare to keep dreaming. Dare to keep living.

Glenn Cunningham was one such person who refused to give up his dreams even when they seemed impossible to achieve:

The little country schoolhouse was heated by an old-fashioned, pot-bellied coal stove. An eight-year-old boy named Glenn Cunningham had the job of coming to school early each day so that he could use kerosene to start the fire and warm the room before his teacher and his classmates arrived. One cold morning someone mistakenly filled the kerosene container he used with gasoline, and disaster struck.

The class and teacher arrived to find the schoolhouse engulfed in flames. Terrified on realizing that Glenn was inside, they rushed in and managed to drag the unconscious little boy out of the flaming building more dead than alive. He had major burns over the lower half of his body and was taken to a nearby county hospital.

From his bed, the dreadfully burned, semi-conscious little boy faintly heard the doctor talking to his mother. The doctor told his mother that her son would surely die – which was for the best, really – for the terrible fire had devastated the lower half of his body.

But the brave boy didn't want to die. Glenn made up his mind that he would survive. And somehow, to the amazement of the physician, he did survive. Yet when the mortal danger was past, he again heard the doctor and his mother speaking quietly. His mother was told that since the fire had destroyed so much flesh in the lower part of his body, he was doomed to be a lifetime cripple with no use at all of his lower limbs. He had lost all the flesh on his knees and shins and all the toes on his left foot. Also, his transverse arch was practically destroyed. But against the doctor's advice, his mother refused to let them amputate.

Once more this brave little boy made up his mind. He would not be a cripple. He would walk. But unfortunately from the waist down, Glenn had no motor ability. His thin, scarred legs just dangled there, all but lifeless.

Ultimately Glenn was released from the hospital. Every day afterward his mother and father would massage his little legs, but there was no feeling, no control, nothing. Yet his determination that he would walk was as strong as ever.

When he wasn't in bed, he was confined to a wheelchair. One sunny day his mother wheeled him out into the yard to get some fresh air. This day, instead of sitting there, he threw himself from the chair. Glenn pulled himself across the grass, dragging his legs behind him.

He worked his way to the white picket fence bordering their lot. With great effort, he raised himself up on the fence. Then, stake by stake, he began dragging himself along the fence, resolved that he would walk. He started to do this every day until he wore a smooth path all around the yard beside the fence. There was nothing he wanted more than to develop life in those legs.

Ultimately through his daily massages, Glenn's iron persistence and his resolute determination, he did develop the ability to stand up. Then in the summer of 1919 - two years after the accident, he took his first halting steps with help, then eventually he was able to walk by himself – and then miraculously – he began to run.

He had a positive attitude as well as a strong faith. His favourite Bible verse was Isaiah 40:31: *"But those who wait on the Lord shall renew their strength; they shall mount up with wings like eagles, they shall run and not be weary, they shall walk and not faint."* 23

Glenn began to run to school. He ran for the sheer joy of running and being able to run. He ran everywhere that he could. The people in his town would often see him run by on his way to who knows where and smile. Later in college Glenn made the track team where his tremendous determination paid off. He eventually received the nickname the "Kansas Flyer".

In February 1934, in New York City's famed Madison Square Garden, this young man who was not expected to survive, who would surely never walk, who could never hope to run – this determined young man, Dr. Glenn Cunningham, ran the mile in four minutes and eight seconds, the world's fastest indoor mile! Later that same year in a prestigious outdoor track meet, he shaved another second off his record to run the world's fastest mile to that time. In 1938, he set a world record in the indoor mile run of 4:04.4. He finally retired from competition in 1940 at the age of thirty-one. (Glenn's record stood for sixteen years till Roger Bannister was the first to break the four-minute mile, in 1954.) 24

Glenn Cunningham fell countless times while he fought to regain the use of his legs. But he didn't focus on the pain of falling - he focused on picking himself back up again. Whatever dream you want to achieve, you are going to fall many times before you finally realize it.

Don't let the pain of a fall or even many falls keep you down. Get up and try again.

You may think you are young and that you have all the time in the world to do the things you dream of doing. Take a word of advice from the iconic actor, James Dean, who died suddenly at the age of twenty-four in a car accident:

"Dream as if you'll live forever. Live as if you'll die today." 25

Today is the day to pursue your dreams - you are not guaranteed tomorrow.

You may be older and feel that life has passed you by. You may have settled for a mundane existence and think you're too old to follow your long forgotten dreams. Think again....

At forty-two, Kareem Abdul-Jabbar became the oldest regular NBA player.

At forty-six, Jack Nicklaus became the oldest man ever to win the Masters.

At forty-nine, Julia Child published her book *Mastering the Art of French Cooking.*

At fifty-five, Pablo Picasso completed his masterpiece *Guernica.*

At sixty-two, J.R.R. Tolkien published the first volume of his fantasy series *Lord of the Rings.*

At sixty-five, just weeks before he died, jazz musician Miles Davis defiantly performed his final live album.

At sixty-six, Noah Webster completed his monumental *American Dictionary of the English Language.*

At sixty-nine, Canadian Ed Whitlock of Milton, Ontario, Canada, became the oldest person to run a standard marathon in under three hours (2:52:47).

At seventy-one, Katsusuke Yanagisawa, a retired Japanese school-teacher, became the oldest person to climb Mt. Everest.

At seventy-five, cancer survivor Barbara Hillary became one of the oldest people and the first black woman to reach the North Pole.

At seventy-seven, John Glenn became the oldest person to go into space.

At eighty, Christine Brown of Laguna Hills, CA, flew to China and climbed the Great Wall.

At eighty-two, William Ivy Baldwin became the oldest tightrope walker, crossing the South Boulder Canyon in Colorado on a three hundred-twenty foot wire.

At eighty-five, Theodor Mommsen became the oldest person to receive a Nobel Prize in Literature.

At eighty-six, Katherine Pelton swam the 200-metre butterfly in 3 minutes, 1.14 seconds, beating the men's world record for that age group by over 20 seconds.

At eighty-eight, Michelangelo created the architectural plans for the Church of Santa Maria degli Angeli.

At ninety-one, Allan Stewart of New South Wales completed a Bachelor of Law degree from the University of New England.

At ninety-two, Paul Spangler finished his fourteenth marathon.

At ninety-three, P.G. Wodehouse worked on his ninety-seventh novel, was knighted, and died.

At ninety-four, comedian George Burns performed in Schenectady, NY, sixty-three years after his first performance there.

At ninety-five, Nola Ochs became the oldest person to receive a college diploma.

At ninety-six, Harry Bernstein published his first book entitled *The Invisible Wall*. He had started writing three years prior to cope with loneliness after Ruby, his wife of seventy years, passed away.

At one hundred, Frank Schearer was the oldest active water skier in the world. *26*

There are no reasons for not pursuing your passion - only excuses. Now I want to challenge you: What would you do with your life; what would you attempt to achieve; who would you aspire to be; if you believed it was impossible to fail? Dare to dream. Dare to become the person of your dreams.

> *It will be in the pursuit of your dreams that*
> *you will discover who you really are.*

Conclusion - Stand Up for Yourself

At the beginning of this discourse we recalled how the television game show *To Tell the Truth* always concluded with the host saying, *"Will the real (person) please stand up?"* Thereupon the true individual would stand and reveal himself.

As our journey together through this book comes to an end, I hope you have come to a revelation of your true self and that you are now empowered to stand up - stand up for your true self, stand up for your dreams, stand up for your uniqueness. May you find it intolerable to sit complacently any longer with all the limitations and excuses of the past that have kept you living below your potential.

"Remember always that you not only have the right to be an individual, you have an obligation to be one." 1

Eleanor Roosevelt

May this book serve not only to encourage you with the limitless potential of your identity, but also impress upon you the absolute necessity of the task. Simply stated: *If you won't be you, who will?* The world is literally dying for individuals who are authentically themselves.

African American author and civil rights leader Howard W. Thurman so aptly said:

> *"Don't ask yourself what the world needs, ask yourself what makes you come alive. And then go and do that. Because what the world needs is people who have come alive."* 2

I believe if you will apply what you have learned in this book, you will come alive - alive to new possibilities, new opportunities, new passion, and new dreams. Now that you have been awakened, continue to build and challenge your new identity.

You have only just scratched the surface - so much is yet to be discovered. Understanding and becoming your best self is a lifelong journey. Keep moving forward. Rather than one giant explosion of light, your identity will, like the dawn, grow gradually brighter with each purposeful step you take.

I invite you to embark upon the adventure of a lifetime - discover and enjoy your true identity. Become who you were destined to be. It's time to let the real me stand up!

Endnotes

INTRODUCTION

1. https://en.wikipedia.org/wiki/To_Tell_the_Truth
2. http://en.wikipedia.org/wiki/Seed_dormancy

CHAPTER ONE

1. *Switch on Your Brain,* Baker Books 2013, P.O. Box 6287, Grand Rapids, MI 49516-6287 pg. 140.
2. *Collins English Dictionary* - Complete & Unabridged 10th Edition 2009 © William Collins Sons & Co. Ltd. 1979, 1986 © HarperCollins Publishers 1998, 2000, 2003, 2005, 2006, 2007, 2009 Cite This Source.
3. http://www.thefreedictionary.com/DNA
4. http://en.wikipedia.org/wiki/DNA
5. The Holy Bible, New King James Version®. Copyright © 1982 by Thomas Nelson. Used by permission. All rights reserved.
6. The Holy Bible, Contemporary English Version, Copyright © 1995 by American Bible Society.
7. Amplified Bible, Classic Edition (AMPC) Copyright © 1954, 1958, 1962, 1964, 1965, 1987 by The Lockman Foundation.

8. Amplified Bible, Classic Edition (AMPC) Copyright © 1954, 1958, 1962, 1964, 1965, 1987 by The Lockman Foundation.
9. http://www.theguardian.com/childrens-books-site/2014/aug/26/top-10-quotes-on-identity-for-teenagers-george-r-r-martin
10. http://www.wisdomquotes.com/quote/anne-lamott-1.html

CHAPTER TWO

1. *Flying Closer to the Flame*, Published July 1st 1993 by W Publishing Group https://books.google.ca/books?id=Mm_U1VqZ9qoC&pg=PT170&lpg=PT170&dq=Ah,+if+that+cosmonaut+had+stepped+out+of+his+spacesuit,+he+would+have+seen+God!"&source=bl&ots=BR25YqtLKk&sig=jPM682C6CKcaDZ6Iu6g1pUX7qfw&hl=en&sa=X&ved=0ahUKEwjHoq_Li5HKAhUO-GMKHVmhC_UQ6AEIHDAA#v=onepage&q=Ah%2C%20if%20that%20cosmonaut%20had%20stepped%20out%20of%20his%20spacesuit%2C%20he%20would%20have%20seen%20God!"&f=false
2. http://www.thegoodliemovie.com
3. *The American Heritage® Stedman's Medical Dictionary* Copyright © 2002, 2001, 1995 by Houghton Mifflin Company. Published by Houghton Mifflin Company.
4. http://www.goodreads.com/quotes/tag/deep-thoughts

CHAPTER THREE

1. http://www.crimelibrary.com/criminal_mind/psychology/kenneth_parnell/6.html
2. Steven%20Stayner%20-%20Wikipedia,%20the%20free%20encyclopedia.webarchive
3. https://answers.yahoo.com/question/index?qid=20060901115953AAM38Uo
4. http://www.money-zine.com/career-development/finding-a-job/getting-fired/

5.http://www.sciencedaily.com/releases/2012/06/120612101338.htm?utm_source=rss&utm_medium=rss&utm_campaign=a-fathers-love-is-one-of-the-greatest-influences-on-personality-development

6. A. Khaleque, R. P. Rohner. (2011). Transnational relations between perceived parental acceptance and personality dispositions of children and adults: A meta-analytic review. *Personality and Social Psychology Review, 16*(2): 103. DOI: 10.1177/1088868311418986

7. John Fuhrman, *Reject me I Love It,* Revised 2nd Edition, Possibility Press 2012, pg. 58.

8 http://www.goodreads.com/quotes/142758-pain-is-inevitable-suffering-is-optional

9. John Fuhrman, *Reject me I Love It,* Revised 2nd Edition, Possibility Press 2012, pg. 22, 23.

10. http://www.brainyquote.com/quotes/quotes/s/sylvesters141898.html#kPVMgPZXByDOYV0f.99

11. http://www.brainyquote.com/quotes/quotes/des-mondtut454129.html#dxudHWTG1pdpmp3R.99

12. http://www.brainyquote.com/quotes/quotes/r/roberthsc156006.html#jbKj5g4Kx8IjtM1i.99

13. Dr. James B. Richards, *How to Stop the Pain,* Whitaker House 2001, 30 Hunt Valley Circle, New Kensington, PA 15068, page 93, 94.

14. http://www.brainyquote.com/quotes/quotes/t/tobykeith177178.html#VsJVIdJX5qkZowrx.99

15. http://www.brainyquote.com/quotes/quotes/j/janisjopli163010.html#maGiifpFttFeC2FH.99

CHAPTER FOUR

1. https://www.goodreads.com/author/quotes/12080.Ralph_Waldo_Emerson

2. David Eckman, *Knowing the Heart of the Father,* Harvest House 2008, Eugene, Oregon 97402, pg. 107.

3. David Eckman, *Knowing the Heart of the Father*, Harvest House 2008, Eugene, Oregon 97402, pg. 108.
4. http://www.scientificamerican.com/article/elephants-never-forget/
5. http://www.upali.ch/training_en.html
6. http://www.onekind.org/be_inspired/top_10_lists/strongest/
7. http://www.wildlife-pictures-online.com/african-elephant.html
8. Word for Today, copyright 2011 Bob Gass Ministries Box 769030, Roswell Georgia 30076, USA
9. http://www.goodreads.com/quotes/tag/overcoming
10. http://www.italianrenaissance.org/michelangelos-david/

CHAPTER FIVE

1. http://www.goodreads.com/author/show/38285.C_G_Jung
2. http://en.wikipedia.org/wiki/Mistaken_identity
3. http://en.wikipedia.org/wiki/Mistaken_identity
4. Brené Brown, http://www.goodreads.com/quotes/tag/authenticity
5. Drs. Hal and Sidra Stone, *Embracing Your Inner Critic*, Harper One a division of Harper Collins Publishers 1993, pg. 24.
6. Thom Rutledge, *Self-Forgiveness Handbook*, New Harbinger Publications Inc. 1997, pg. 2.
7. http://www.positivityblog.com/index.php/2014/03/19/self-esteem-quotes/
8. Dr. David Hawkins, *Dealing with the CrazyMakers in Your Life*, Harvest House Publishers 2007, pg. 196-197.
9. http://www.goodreads.com/quotes/tag/self-esteem

CHAPTER SIX

1.Holy Bible. New Living Translation copyright© 1996, 2004, 2007, 2013 by Tyndale House Foundation. Used by permission of Tyndale House Publishers Inc., Carol Stream, Illinois 60188.
2. *Self Talk 101: Why You Need To Believe In Yourself* by Jim Jensen http://inspiyr.com/the-incredible-power-of-self-talk/

3. Dr. Caroline Leaf, *Switch on Your Brain,* 2013 Baker Books, a division of Baker Publishing Group, P.O. Box 6287, Grand Rapids, MI 49516-6287, pg. 34-36
4. http://www.goodreads.com/author/show/7242192.Maddy_Malhotra
5. Maddy Malhotra, *How to Build Self-Esteem and Be Confident: Overcome Fears, Break Habits, Be Successful and Happy* http://www.goodreads.com/quotes/tag/self-talk
6. http://www.goodreads.com/quotes/tag/self-talk
7. Joyce Meyer, *Living Beyond Your Feelings,* Pg 184,185, 2001 Faith words Hachette Book Group, 237 Park Ave. New York, NY 10017.
8. http://www.goodreads.com/quotes/tag/emotion
9. http://www.goodreads.com/quotes/tag/self-esteem
10. Dr. James B. Richards, *How to Stop the Pain,* Whitaker House 2001, 30 Hunt Valley Circle, New Kensington, PA 15068.

CHAPTER SEVEN

1. http://conversationswithcynthia.com/category/self-improvement/
2. Dr. James B. Richards, *How to Stop the Pain,* Whitaker House 2001, 30 Hunt Valley Circle, New Kensington, PA 15068, pg. 62.
3. http://www.goodreads.com/quotes/tag/perception
4. Dr. James B. Richards - *Escape from Co-Dependent Christianity,* Impact International Publications, 3300 N. Broad Place SW, Huntsville, AL 35805 1996 , ch. 9 pg. 2.
5. Joyce Meyer, *Battlefield of the Mind Devotional,* 2005, Faith Words Hachette Book Group 237 Park Ave. New York, NY 10017, pg. 27, 28.
6. http://www.positivityblog.com/index.php/2014/03/19/self-esteem-quotes/

CHAPTER EIGHT

1. http://en.wikipedia.org/wiki/The_Lion_King
2. http://www.brainyquote.com/quotes/quotes/a/arnoldhgl105231.html#RoGAyBqvhzYjDm5u.99
3.Holy Bible. New Living Translation copyright© 1996, 2004, 2007, 2013 by Tyndale House Foundation. Used by permission of Tyndale House Publishers Inc., Carol Stream, Illinois 60188.
4. http://www.brainyquote.com/quotes/quotes/b/bernardmel157507.html#FW8IpgI8tqTGR9Iy.99
5. http://www.brainyquote.com/quotes/quotes/j/johnfkenn121400.html#vjSF7c5l1fsvko8r.99
6. http://www.brainyquote.com/quotes/quotes/d/deniswaitl146912.html#1LvYZ0OjWo5MfXMJ.99
7. Bob Gass, Copyright 2011 Bob Gass Ministries, Roswell Georgia, USA *The Word for You Today* Dec Jan Feb 2012, pg. 34.
8. http://www.goodreads.com/quotes/tag/courage
9. http://www.goodreads.com/quotes/tag/courage
10. Bob Gass, Copyright 2011 Bob Gass Ministries, Roswell Georgia, USA, *The Word for You Today* Dec Jan Feb 2012, pg. 50.
11. Joyce Meyer, *The Confident Woman Devotional*, 2011, Faith Words, Hachette Book Group, 237 Park Avenue, New York, NY 10017.
12. http://www.brainyquote.com/quotes/quotes/e/eleanorroo141470.html#Rddy6L2jSpxHsaCU.99
13. Joyce Meyer, *God is Not Mad at You*, Faith Words 2013, Hachette Book Group, 237 Park Avenue, New York, NY 10017, pg. 45.
14. http://en.wikipedia.org/wiki/Koi
15. Bob Gass, Copyright 2011 Bob Gass Ministries, Roswell Georgia, USA, *The Word for you Today*, Dec Jan Feb 2012, pg. 39.
16. http://dictionary.reference.com/browse/complacency?s=t
17. http://www.goodreads.com/quotes/tag/complacency
18. http://www.goodreads.com/quotes/tag/victory In "Blood, Toil, Tears, and Sweat," his first speech as Prime Minister to the House of Commons May 13,1940 quoted by Jeffrey

R. Holland in "However Long and Hard the Road" BYU Devotional 18 Jan 1983" Winston S. Churchill.

CHAPTER NINE

1. http://www.thefarside.com
2. http://psychcentral.com/lib/what-is-a-trigger/0001414
3. Eckhart Tolle, *A New Earth: Awakening to Your Life's Purpose* http://www.goodreads.com/quotes/tag/reaction?page=3
4. J. John and Mark Stibbe, *A Barrel of Fun*, West Sussex, England: Monarch, 2004, pg. 76-77.
5. Bryant McGill, *Simple Reminders: Inspiration for Living Your Best Life* http://www.goodreads.com/quotes/tag/reaction?page=3
6. http://www.stevemaraboli.com/Motivational-Quotes.html

CHAPTER TEN

1. http://socialwork.buffalo.edu/resources/self-care-starter-kit/introduction-to-self-care.html#title_6
2. http://socialwork.buffalo.edu/resources/self-care-starter-kit/introduction-to-self-care.html#title_6
3. RAINN.org http://www.uky.edu/StudentAffairs/VIPCenter/downloads/self%20care%20defined.pdf
4. http://www.csep.ca/CMFiles/Guidelines/CanadianPhysicalActivityGuidelinesStatements_E.pdf
5. http://www.quotegarden.com/stress.html
6. http://www.cancercenter.com/treatments/laughter-therapy/
7. Read more at: http://www.azquotes.com/quote/1423876
8. Some information adapted from RAINN.org, UK Violence Intervention and Prevention Program.
9. http://mainstreetvegan.net/about-us/
10. http://www.goodreads.com/quotes/tag/self-care
11. http://internal-acceptance-movement.tumblr.com/aboutme
12. http://www.goodreads.com/quotes/tag/self-care

CHAPTER ELEVEN

1. https://www.pinterest.com/explore/identity-quotes/
2. http://www.strokeassociation.org/STROKEORG/LifeAfterStroke/InspirationalStories/AHAASA-Past-President-Shares-Stroke-Survival-Story_UCM_452135_Article.jsp
3. http://www.positivityblog.com/index.php/2014/03/19/self-esteem-quotes/
4. Gary Collins, *Christian Counselling* 3rd Edition, Thomas Nelson, 2007, pg. 433-440.
5. http://www.brainyquote.com/quotes/quotes/c/carljung132738.html
6. http://www.goodreads.com/quotes/9650-remember-you-have-been-criticizing-yourself-for-years-and-it
7. http://www.goodreads.com/quotes/tag/goals-in-life
8. http://www.goodreads.com/quotes/tag/negativity?page=2 *E-Go: Ego Distancing Through Mindfulness, Emotional Intelligence, and the Language of Love.*
9. http://www.goodreads.com/quotes/tag/negativity?page=2
10. Read more at http://www.brainyquote.com/quotes/quotes/t/tonicollet432036.html#fWmYjGp0YUeqjEdP.99
11. http://www.goodreads.com/quotes/tag/adventure
12. http://www.calebwojcik.com/blog/2012/01/30/quotes-overcome-fear-of-failure
13. Michael Jordan, National Basketball Association. Retrieved January 15, 2007. http://en.wikipedia.org/wiki/Michael_Jordan#cite_note-nbah-3
14. http://www.calebwojcik.com/blog/2012/01/30/quotes-overcome-fear-of-failure
15. http://www.goodreads.com/quotes/tag/giving
16. https://en.wikipedia.org/wiki/Johannes_Gutenberg
17. https://en.wikipedia.org/wiki/Mother_Teresa
18. "http://www.goodreads.com/quotes/tag/giving
19. http://www.answerbag.com/q_view/2232446

20. http://www.positivityblog.com/index.php/2014/03/19/self-esteem-quotes/
21. http://www.goodreads.com/quotes/tag/dreaming
22. https://www.goodreads.com/author/quotes/249881.Orrin_Woodward
23. https://en.wikipedia.org/wiki/Glenn_Cunningham_(athlete)
24.http://www.wanttoknow.info/050702powerofdetermination
25. Read more at http://www.brainyquote.com/quotes/quotes/j/jamesdean103528.html#UfymoIItPkQl8puW.99
26. Edited excerpt from *Edgy Conversations: How Ordinary People Can Achieve Outrageous Success*. Copyright © 2013 by Daniel E. Waldschmidt. All rights reserved. Read more: http://www.businessinsider.com/100-amazing-accomplishments-achieved-at-every-age-2014-3#ixzz3hQH0Y3rl

CONCLUSION

1. http://www.brainyquote.com/quotes/quotes/e/eleanorroo387005.html
2. http://www.positivityblog.com/index.php/2014/03/19/self-esteem-quotes/

CPSIA information can be obtained
at www.ICGtesting.com
Printed in the USA
LVOW04s0021250716
497015LV00006B/1/P

9 781773 020990